Adva

MW00365835

Applause... simple and yet so profound
"This book is pure genius: perceptive and profound, yet so simple. It is precisely what American parents need to thwart the millennial malaise. MBA not required; anyone can tell a one-minute story and ask a question. Socrates, Aquinas and grandparents will be applauding."
—Frank A. Benevento II, father, grandfather, and investment banker

A fresh model for thoughtful, ethical decision-making
"There is no more important nor more challenging responsibility for parents than to help our sons and daughters make thoughtful, ethical decisions. Anne provides us an innovative and thoughtful model for guiding our children toward wise decisions. She shows how the case method can tap profoundly into children's imagination, love of story, and natural desire to solve problems and at the same time build their self-awareness, independence, confidence, resilience, and critical thinking skills. Anne's model also serves to strengthen communication and relationships between children and their parents. I urge parents and teachers to read this book's very fresh and creative ideas about helping children become good, prudent, and honest decision-makers."
—Billy Peebles, Headmaster, the Lovett School

Brilliant . . . any parent can do it
"I love this idea! I think I used that approach without even knowing it. I also went to Harvard Business School and must have had it in the back of my mind while raising my son. It works! Now Anne has written the instruction manual on it. It is brilliant, and truly, any parent can do it."
—Lara Hodgson, mother and CEO of NOWaccount

When all else failed... I tried it... and saw the miracle
"I have been in child development for 14 years and have tried every method from timeouts to redirecting. Each child responds differently to different methods. I have found none to be 100% effective or teach wise decision-making from within. Anne encouraged me to try what she was doing with her son. It was a miracle. I noticed that all the children I work with loved my stories, and kept coming back for more. The best part: they were all equally more thoughtful, often stopping to consider their actions. It is truly remarkable to see their brains working not just to avoid being in trouble but taking charge of their actions and how it impacts their own little lives."

—Leslie Gilbeaux, caregiver and owner of Marie Victoria Brides

What a practical approach to character education!
"What a splendid idea, the Harvard way to address what is most important in early childhood, character education! Parents often ignore what is most important at the expense of the urgent rote learning. This is the most ready-to-apply parenting book I have encountered, examples scattered throughout the text. Children who learn how to focus and make wise choices early have an easier time learning organization and time management skills as they grow up."

—Melissa Lowry, mother and education coach

Extends the reach of Harvard Business School learning methods...
"As an MBA from Harvard Business School, I learned the value of telling, listening and participating in a great story (i.e. the case method). The cases taught me how to make decisions and then how to consider living with them. Storytelling is the most impactful, influential, and memorable method of learning. Children love stories, especially if they relate directly to them. Anyone can tell a one-minute story to a child about an event and then ask

what the kid in the scenario should do. It is 'the case method for kids' and every parent should try it."

—Amelia DiVenere, mother and corporate finance executive

Got the hang of it quickly

"I was intrigued about Anne's case method and wanted to try a Harvard-tested approach with my children, unconventional as it was. At first it was hard to keep my stories short enough to keep my children interested, but I got a hang of it pretty quickly. Now I pay more attention to what my young children experience every day, and engaging them with the case stories has brought us closer. My children know I care about them and am interested in their lives. It is a great way to help them grow in wisdom!"

—Abby Moore Elmore, mother & real estate broker

The Case Method Miracle

Guiding Children To Make Wise Decisions The Harvard Business School Way

Anne Ylipahkala Jones

Publisher's Cataloging-in-Publication Data
Names: Jones, Anne Ylipahkala.
Title: The Case method miracle: guiding children to make wise decisions the Harvard Business School way / Anne Ylipahkala Jones.
Description: Atlanta, GA: Crimson Square Press, 2019.
Identifiers: LCCN 2019911197 | ISBN 9781074001827
Subjects: LCSH Parenting. | Parenthood. | Child rearing. | Self-reliance in children. | Child development. | Reinforcement (Psychology) | Decision making. | Harvard Business School. |BISAC FAMILY & RELATIONSHIPS / Parenting / General
Classification: LCC HQ769 .J751 2019 | DDC 649.6--dc23

The information and advice contained in this book are based upon the research and the personal and professional experiences of the author. The information in this book is true and complete to the best of the author's knowledge. Any advice or recommendations are made without guarantee on the part of the author or publisher. The author and publisher disclaim any liability in connection with the use of this information. Although the examples in this book remain factual, certain names and identifying characteristics have been changed to protect the identity and privacy of individuals and their families.

Cover photo by Mark Mitchell Jones.
Book cover design by Anne Ylipahkala Jones.
Author photo by Jupiter Justin Jones.

www.casemethodmiracle.com.

To Jupiter, my love for you gave birth to this idea. You made it alive. You are my Sweet Love.

To Mark, your love and unwavering faith in me purposed me to write this down. You are my Big Love.

Contents

I.

Breakthrough!
A Revolutionary, Simple Way
to Raise Your Child

I cannot teach anybody anything, I can only make them think.
Socrates

1. It's a Miracle!

Children need to be raised. Taught. Guided. Helped to think. And to think wisely. To make decisions that are good, and right. Most parents know these things, but are perplexed, if not paralyzed, by the fundamental question, "How?"

Life assaults us at full speed. In the midst of it we need to figure out how to raise children. Some of us were raised well, and think we can do what our parents did. Others were not raised so well, and think we should *not* raise our children the way we were. Some of us find that what we do doesn't seem to work, or at least not work very well.

I believe there is an easy solution to this problem. It is a simple technique that works in nearly every case, for all kinds of children. This straightforward approach should be an essential key in the toolbox of parenting skills. It is the case method. For many, it is a miracle.

While miracles usually happen just once, the case method is a process that can be applied to countless problems, over and over. I've used it successfully hundreds of times. The case method is a teaching approach that uses decision-forcing situations as guideposts. In the classroom, it puts students in the roles of leaders who were faced with difficult decisions at some time in the past. It is used at leading professional schools such as the Harvard Business School.

I discovered that the case method—telling decision-forcing stories—works with children. They enjoy it and learn from it. Parents can use it without paying hundreds of thousands of dollars in tuition to Harvard! You can acquire this skill in minutes and use it over and over. It can transform how you raise your child.

In this book, I explain how you can use a version of the case method with your child. To make it work for kids, I have stripped it to its bare bones. It is still powerful, yet super simple. Any parent can do it, anytime, anywhere.

Fewer timeouts, yelling and screaming, or telling the child what to do.

The genius in the case method is that it teaches your child to think for himself. Now, a whole lot of the work of raising your child has been moved to the child! He is thinking for himself, not being pushed, cajoled, persuaded, or bribed. Instead of you supplying all the effort, your child is pulling the proverbial oar. Under your expert eye, your child is raising himself and imbedding self-confidence in the process!

As a parent, it is easy to do. Just tell your child a one-minute story about another child in a situation where he has to make a choice. The situation should be a scenario with which your child can identify. "Once there was a little boy…" The boy makes a choice. At the end you ask, "Was that a wise or unwise decision?" Or you ask, "What should the little boy do?" That is the case method, putting the case dilemma to the child to answer. You stop and let it sink in for the child.

The case method *miracle* takes place when the child starts making mindful, wise decisions in his own life, both in situations that resemble told case stories and in those that do not.

The case method is not meant to be the only method for raising your child. You have other tools in your parenting toolbox. It is not an approach to replace your other parenting strategies, but to complement and enhance what you are already doing. Experience shows, however, that it is an invaluable and transformative tool.

It is up to you how often you employ the case method. Every day, once a week, when you are in a difficult spot with your child, or whenever you like. It is up to you whether you make it your main parenting strategy, or whether you use it selectively, on occasions when it suits you and the timing works—in either case it will work and it will help. The case method should not be an added burden, but an alternative to use when you recognize an opening, a simple tool to help your child learn instinctively to think for himself.

Harvard University is often associated with using cases to teach business, law, and government. I went to Harvard Business School where they teach exclusively with the case method. Harvard Business School has been a leading business program in the world since its founding in 1908. The case method may have something to do with it.

The cases at Harvard Business School are descriptions of business circumstances where a business leader has to solve a problem, given the case facts. The students put themselves in the role of that decision-maker when they read the case and come up with solutions. At Harvard Business School they believe the case method is an effective way to prepare students for the challenges of leadership. I believe it is an effective way to prepare children to lead their own lives thoughtfully and responsibly.

But to make it work for children I had to innovate. What I propose is to extrapolate creatively and apply the case method with children in its most simple form, bare bones. I know this adaptation works because I have used it with my son, Jupiter, over and over.

After discovering its power, I started to document the idea. Surely I wasn't the only person using the famous case method with my child. Thousands of Harvard graduates, and students from other schools, had been deeply exposed to the case method. I supposed some of them had used it with children, and perhaps written about it.

I searched the internet for any material or research on doing cases like this with children. To my surprise, I did not find anything. There was nothing about using case stories with preschool and elementary school age children. Some schools had employed the case method with student teams in middle school, more imitating the business school approach to teach a certain principle. Everything relating to the case method described complex decision-making in a classroom setting. What about teaching wisdom, inner grit, leadership, thoughtfulness, honesty, kindness, consideration? In other words, teaching life skills and character traits to children one-on-one with the case method in its simplest form. Specifically, teaching these traits when it matters the most, at the preschool and elementary school age. There was nothing on it on the internet. I felt I had stumbled on a treasure that nobody had thought to pick up and document. Having seen it work, I knew it was my calling to explain the idea and share it so other parents could benefit from it.

As I have applied the case method idea with Jupiter and shared the approach with other parents and caregivers, who in turn have tried it, I have been reassured of its capacity. The case method seems to work even more effectively with children than adult students, almost like a miracle. Children start thinking more on their own and to choosing wisely.

Perhaps this is so because a child's imagination is so powerful that the line between what is real and what is not is blurred. When your child listens to a case story about someone with whom he identifies, it seems that he does a lot more than a twenty-something student reading a business case, who may approach it in quite a detached manner. As he hears your story, your child puts himself in the shoes of the little boy in the case and actually *becomes* that little boy in his mind. Later, when a real dilemma such as the one described in the case presents itself, your child is prepped for the wise course of action. I have seen it work. It is the case method miracle. It can be used by moms, dads, and other caregivers. They can all be miracle workers!

The key outcomes are grit and self-reliance for the child, and mutual bonding between the child and the parent. Thinking through the case and making a judgment or a decision about what the case protagonist should do prepares the child for the same kind of challenges in his life. As the parent or the caregiver affirms the child with hugs and praise, "Great job, you know how to make wise decisions," the child receives the message, "You got it." In addition, rewarding the child with an expression of love capitalizes on the child's most powerful desire, to be loved.

This brief experience—taking less than a minute—strengthens the bond between the child and the parent. The child gains confidence that he has what it takes to handle the situation. It becomes easier for him to stick to what he knows to be wise, and to focus on the task at hand. He becomes more self-reliant and perseveres to stand alone, even passionately, for what he believes is right.

To describe the result of this process, used over and over, I had to revert to my first language, Finnish. In Finland we have a word, *sisu,* which describes the outcome better than any English word, though "grit" comes close. *Sisu* is a fascinating word. Some English language words that express aspects of *sisu* include grit, tenacity, resilience, stoic determination, equanimity, achievement, bravery, courage, and the good life. There is no official definition for it, but you know it when you see it. It is one of my favorite words. The Finns claim to have been born with it; that it is in the national character. However, I think we work it into our character as we tackle challenges and overcome obstacles. We build it in like a muscle.

This book describes how your child can have *sisu.* Or character and grit, if you prefer.

There are four parts to this book. The first part describes *how the case method works* in the parenting setting and how I have employed it. The second part is a guide on *how to build cases* on your own. The third part of the book consists of *example case stories* to get you started on your own. The last part of the book is a *troubleshooting guide.* I put it together from the most common problems I encountered with friends trying the approach.

The cases are simple; that is why they are powerful. Jupiter started calling the cases "wise and unwise decisions." I started calling the whole process "the case method miracle," because it works like magic.

To protect my friends' privacy, I have changed the names in my examples. Throughout this book I have referred to a generic child with "a little boy" or the masculine pronoun "he." I did this to keep consistent and not go back and forth, to avoid the cumbersome interjection of "or little girl" and "or she" throughout the text. My case examples in section three are about a little boy, also for consistency. If you prefer, you can just switch them to "a little girl." The cases are so short it is simple to do. Since I have drawn the examples from my immediate experience, they deal with scenarios a preschool or elementary age child might encounter. Please do not let this limit you. As you engage your older child with case stories, you only have to relate with circumstances relevant to your child. Naturally, the older the child, the longer the case can be, the more nuanced and complicated to accommodate for your child's maturity level. The key constructs, however, remain the same, to keep the stories focused, relatable, and to reward your child for knowing the wise way to go.

2. Birth of the Idea

Going all out and keeping it simple

The way I approached parenting was the way I approach everything in my life. I go all out and I keep it simple. I never do ten things at a time, I do one or two. I take a look, explore a bit more, and then if it is something I want to try, I jump in with all I have. Then I focus on a couple of simple things I can handle. The "whatever you do, do it with all your might" attitude, and my deep desire for simplicity, were major contributors that gave birth to the simplified case method for children.

At each turning point, focus carried me forward

I grew up in Finland. I was joyful and full of play during my early childhood. Then, in elementary school, I received a 4/10 grade for a math test. I had not been focused. I was still playing too much, scattered, not focused on school. The grade was a fail. And a shock.

That one test and my failing grade became a turning point. I determined not to get such a grade again. I worked hard on homework to master every subject. I started receiving more A's and graduated from high school as valedictorian.

When I first came to America as an exchange student, it did not work out so well. The family with whom I stayed thought I was an oddity. I ate tomatoes like apples (I had never seen them growing outside the way they did in Atlanta, so I picked them as if from an apple tree), I was not interested in boys or partying, and I read *Track & Field News* instead of the magazines other girls my age were reading. I started feeling like a misfit. In fact I was, at least according to the common standard. I feared the host family was going to ship me back to Finland. In fact, they did ask me to leave. I was nearly consumed with a sense of failure.

The area coordinator for the exchange program took me to stay at her house while she looked for another placement.

I spent my time reading the morning newspaper, working to improve my English. I discovered an article about Georgia Tech having just hired a coach, Dee Todd, to build the women's track program. A glimmer of light; there was one thing I knew I could do. I could run. Even though I had not amounted to much on the national level in Finland, I had worked hard my teen years to build my endurance and running form for middle distance racing. Coach Todd had a solid sprinter squad, but it seemed she could do with some strengthening in the middle distance crew.

The next step was visiting the Athletic Association at Georgia Tech. I found Coach Todd's office, knocked on the door, introduced myself, and asked if I could contribute. Coach Dee Todd invited me in. We talked. She trusted me when I told her my best times and my academic credentials from Finland. She offered me a full scholarship on the spot. I forever will remember her response: "It is the attitude, not the aptitude, which determines the altitude."

I was determined to live up to her confidence in me and ultimately became the top miler in the Atlantic Coast Conference. Notwithstanding the rigors of practice and competition, I did not sacrifice academics and graduated with highest distinction in systems engineering. All those endless running workouts in my teens in the snow and wet of the Finnish roads paid off.

My next project was my work. I went all out to improve the approach to the consulting assignments I had at my first two jobs.

With progressively more challenging assignments, I realized an advanced business degree was necessary to move ahead at the firm. I researched the best business programs and their selection criteria. Harvard Business School was the right fit. First, it was the number one MBA program in the world, and second, they did not require the applicants to take the GMAT, a standardized test required by all the other MBA programs. Resounding in my mind was the Georgia Tech registrar relating my abysmal SAT results. Fortunately, the Georgia Tech track coach had a lot of influence over that situation! So I decided to apply to but one MBA program—Harvard. I was accepted. There are times when it pays to put all my eggs in one basket.

At Harvard Business School I had my awakening to the complexities of business situations via the case method. The two years at Harvard were challenging for me. As an engineer I tended to be introspective and thoughtful. I preferred to study and contemplate rather than to discuss and debate ideas in front of the professor and ninety classmates. It was intimidating, and it was hard for me to think on my feet and present ideas I did not consider well-prepared. Yet I improved steadily during those two years; especially important was learning to contribute in the business setting. It was an invaluable learning experience.

My life was my work those years after business school. Well into my thirties, I started picturing myself as a fifty-year-old executive with ten cats and no family. Was that where I was headed? It was not the future I wanted. It was not why I had come to America. Something was missing. Since it seemed to me that I was not able to balance work with anything else in my life, I decided to drop the fulltime job for something part-time and concentrate on meeting new people. I had savings, and I could quit the high-pressure job.

A year into it I met Mark who later became my husband. It was love at first sight. He picked me up while I was running. He pulled over in his car, rolled down the window with a Coke in his hand. "Want a Diet Coke?" he smiled. Mark was the real thing. I set out to love him and to help him with his medical practice. It was a challenge since I knew nothing about medicine. We turned around the practice by modernizing some aspects of it and reassessing the business strategies and operations.

Motherhood challenged me to keep it simple

Becoming a mom changed me more than any previous event in my life. I had gone all out to be the best wife I could. Now I went all out to be the best mother I could, too. Everything else was by the wayside.

I read parenting books and even took a parenting course. The parenting course was a highly applauded mini-course at my son's pre-school. I liked the idea behind it and the many examples we were given, but I still found the solutions hard to apply. I kept forgetting what I was to do and how I was supposed to respond in the everyday pop-up situations. In addition, I participated in a parenting book study where we discussed issues related to raising children. More than anything, I learned that there were as many approaches as there were mothers in the room. There were no simple solutions to the dilemmas we faced with our children.

Some of the parenting books I read were helpful with a few good ideas. I have some keepers on my bookshelf. On the other hand, many of the books I read left me uncertain about my parenting skills. Have you ever bought a book and thought it would help you solve some of your parenting challenges, only to be left more confused in the end? Or read a book that gave you nothing specific to apply to the dilemmas with your particular child? Perhaps you read—as I did—so many books you were not sure which approach was the best one for you and your family? Or maybe you never read any parenting books because you consider all of them just the flavor of the day or the so-called experts pushing their views? Since when does one need a PhD to offer legitimate, effective ideas on how to raise children?

Similarities between the parenting dilemmas and the Harvard Business School cases

The experience of feeling overwhelmed and being surrounded by ambiguity was familiar to me. It was the way I had felt when I first started at Harvard Business School.

The teaching was accomplished with case studies, and there never was a clear, right answer. It was unsettling.

As an undergraduate, I had studied engineering and mathematics at Georgia Tech. Math is straightforward. You lay out your assumptions and the unchanging laws that apply to the problem. You explain the known constants and known and unknown variables. Finally, you solve the problem for the unknown. There is a correct answer. I could always know whether I solved a problem correctly, or not. There was no "maybe."

In contrast, at Harvard Business School, the problem-solving did not work that way. The cases were descriptions of business situations with a dilemma of what the case protagonist should do in the end. We studied varied, real life business situations, and there were many solutions—most of them good—to each one. The case method teaches students by making the student the decision-maker. Often the information in the case was imperfect and inadequate, and I was trying to make a recommendation with no prior experience handling the kind of a matter illustrated in the case. It was helpful to talk with other students for their perspectives, but I found the process—especially in the beginning—a bit uncomfortable. There was so much ambiguity about the solution, and so many good—if not exactly right—answers. Sometimes even a poor answer was acceptable as long as the student expressed it eloquently with some backup data. It was like parenting.

Once I was a parent, I found myself comparing what was similar and what was different about the two experiences. Both the business and the parenting dilemmas tend to be ambiguous. The Harvard Business School approach was to help the students solve business problems via the case method. Instead of telling them what to do, the school pushed students to think for themselves. I thought that perhaps the case method could apply in the parenting setting by getting children to think for themselves. If I could learn to do it, maybe Jupiter could!

I fashioned Jupiter as the student, while I acted as the professor

What if Jupiter could learn decision-making via cases from *his* immediate life experiences? *Why not?* I could relate a simplified Harvard case method to a different setting and experiment with it. Instead of complicated business situations, my cases would be simple scenarios from Jupiter's daily life. But, the principles of thinking through a solution to a scenario, and learning from it, would remain.

I figured that even though I wasn't a Harvard Business School professor, I was a parent and certainly capable of describing a straightforward life incident to Jupiter. The incidents in Jupiter's life would be the "cases." My cases would be so plain I could tell them on the fly. In my cases I would be comparable to the professor facilitating the case discussion at business school. Jupiter would be the student.

My cases would not be complicated twenty-page business descriptions with a multitude of details and considerations like those at Harvard. Rather, they would be one-minute accounts of something Jupiter had recently experienced or portrayals of familiar situations. Just as I had had to put myself in the shoes of the decision-maker in the business school cases, Jupiter would have to put himself in the shoes of the little boy in the case.

No problem, for don't all children love stories? It made sense for me to try this, especially since I believed Jupiter would enjoy it.

I was pretty sure it would work because it appealed to Jupiter's imagination. I thought a three-year-old would certainly identify with a little boy or a girl in a story more powerfully than a twenty-four-year-old identified with a CEO of a huge business. In fact, children have such amazing imaginations they often have difficulty separating what is real from what is not. I realized this would be helpful in using the case method with children. It works when a person can put himself in another's shoes—and make a judgment about what should be done—so I supposed it would work even better with children given their inherent imaginations.

At Harvard it was the teacher who chose each case for the purpose of drawing out a certain principle that the teacher wanted the students to master. In the same way, as a parent, I could pick the idea I wanted to get across to Jupiter, and focus the case dilemma on that issue. I could do exactly what the professors had done at business school—use cases from countless scenarios to introduce the values I deemed important for Jupiter to master.

Jupiter and I ran with the idea

I began exploring the idea with my three-year-old. I made the experience attractive to him. We cuddled on the sofa. I looked Jupiter in the eyes and told him about a little boy who made a decision. Say, a little boy who was playing in his play area when his mommy came to tell him it was time to take a bath and get ready for bed. The little boy responded, "Yes, Mommy!" Then I asked Jupiter: "Was that a wise decision?" Of course he knew it was. I proceeded to tickle and hug him as a reward. I said, "Good job! You know how to make wise decisions!"

We started out that simple. Jupiter did not even have to come up with any solutions, all he had to do was to recognize whether the little boy in the story made a wise or unwise decision. Instead of using wise and unwise as the choice, I could have as easily used something else, say good and bad, right or wrong, or some similar characterization antipodes. You can use whatever you prefer.

I knew I was on to something when Jupiter came to me the next day and asked if we could do "wise and unwise decisions." He wanted to cuddle on the sofa, too. We did, and he wanted more of the wise and unwise decision stories the next day, and the next. Jupiter loved my telling him stories and holding him. This is how I started the cases, it was that simple. The process evolved from there.

Initially, I used the case story times to teach Jupiter basic good manners; for example, when we say "thank you" and "please." Soon we moved on to what it means to obey fully, when and how we share with other children, how we respond wisely when someone is unkind to us, and how we put things back where they belong.

Here's an example of how it worked in the early days.

We ate dinner together as a family, but Jupiter usually finished eating before Mark and me. He was about three years old, and we thought it was alright for him to play while we finished our meals. However, we did not want Jupiter to leave the table as he pleased without politely excusing himself. I decided to take up the matter of "leaving the dinner table early" with Jupiter. My natural instinct, without thinking about it from a "case" perspective, would have been to tell him what to do, "Please ask to be excused before leaving the table. You shouldn't leave abruptly."

But, I was intent to see how the case method would work. Instead of telling Jupiter what to do, I wanted to try letting him decide how he would handle the situation. So I told him the following case: "Come, let me tell you about a little boy. This little boy was eating dinner with his mommy and daddy. He had his own special plate with pictures of trains and cars. He also had his own fork and spoon. They had animal shapes on them. They were just right for his hands. His daddy was asking him about the new book he loved. The little boy was learning how to talk. He had finished eating his spaghetti and meatballs. Then mommy and daddy started talking with each other. The little boy was not hungry any more. He was ready to play. He wanted to leave the table. He remembered he should say something. He stopped to think. Then he said, 'Mommy, may I be excused?'"

I looked at Jupiter, paused for a second, and posed this question to him: "Was that a wise or unwise decision?" Of course, Jupiter knew the answer. I said, "Great job! The little boy made a wise decision, asking to be excused before jumping off the dinner table." I hugged him and kissed him, telling him how much I loved him. Knowing how to excuse himself politely was one of the few exemplary manners he had at dinner table for a period. I knew there was plenty room for more case stories!

We were encouraged from our initial learnings, which spurred us forward

In the beginning it took more time to use a case story than if I had just told Jupiter to do something, to obey me, especially when it was a straightforward behavior. But he loved the stories, and it was easy to share them with him. Also, I thought it was a good timing to help him start developing self-reliance and strength of character. The genius of this was not that I was teaching Jupiter self-reliance and character, but that *the way* I was teaching him things he needed to learn helped to develop character. This was an added bonus to my efforts at child rearing.

I realized that when I came alongside Jupiter in his life via these cases, it made a difference to him. He respected me more. He loved me more for loving him like that. I could tell our wise and unwise decision times on the sofa were making a difference in more than one way. It was strengthening our relationship in a positive way. Mutual bonding was an unintended positive outcome.

As I continued engaging with Jupiter, I began to see the impact the case stories had on him. Jupiter quickly picked up on the terminology of "making wise and unwise decisions," and I observed him doing himself what he had chosen for the little boy in the case. I noticed it on the playground when he was playing with his friends. My three-year-old was standing up for what he believed was the wise decision when the other boys ran off to mischief—probably not thinking much at all about what was wise or unwise. Jupiter did not even know I was watching them. He did not do it to please me, he made the decision by himself and for himself. I was stunned. I was observing the case method miracle first hand.

I realized I had stumbled upon a treasure

I searched the internet for any material or research on doing cases like this with children. Google can find anything, right? To my surprise, I did not discover anything. Certainly some parents were doing what I was doing, but nobody had written about it. Everything relating to the case method described complex decision-making in a classroom setting. What about teaching wisdom, inner grit, leadership, thoughtfulness, honesty, kindness, consideration? What about teaching life skills to children with the case method in its simplest form? Google let me down.

So, I felt I had stumbled upon a treasure. It seemed as though there had been a gold nugget on the road for decades, and everyone was just walking past it. Now I had found it! I'd discovered that a technique that had been applied successfully to business and law education for decades, was valuable to teach little children.

Clearly, I had streamlined the case method to its bare bones, but the principle was the same. At business school the case method yields students who are confident in expressing their ideas and solutions to their colleagues and bosses, and who can work with others to find ever better alternatives. When employed in a parenting setting, the case method yields children who gain confidence in their ability to handle everyday life scenarios wisely and who develop trust with their parents to be "in it with them." And the method helps children start to develop inner grit and self-reliance while bonding with their parents at an early age.

As children grow older they are bombarded with choices between good and excellent, temptations to waste time, distractions, and lures to risky behaviors. As parents, we cannot always be there to help them navigate this galaxy of choices. I feel it is very important for my child to have inner grit and independent decision-making ability. This is what the case method miracle achieves.

As I continued telling Jupiter wise and unwise decision stories, I discovered that applying the case method in its simplest form to some parenting issues is a breakthrough method. It is immensely versatile and applies to many situations with my child. I do not need to understand every parenting approach and philosophy, all I need to know is what I believe and want for Jupiter and then apply the case method to teach those values. Simply put, just like Harvard Business School believes the case method is the best way to prepare students for the challenges of leadership, I have come to believe the same method works the same way, if not better, with children to prepare them to make wise decisions in their lives.

Really? Yes.

I concluded keeping this to myself would not help anyone, I must share what I have learned

That is how my idea to apply the case method with children was born. After a while I shared it with friends and they started to use it. They had the same success. Once I witnessed how it worked with Jupiter and with my friends' children, I felt compelled to share what I had learned. I wanted to write a book to explain what I have found to be a powerful tool for teaching children wisdom and independent decision-making. To help children start taking charge of their destinies. There is so much at stake.

I then was faced with the question, "Who are *you* to write about raising children? You do not have *any* background or education in psychology and child development. You are only rearing *one* child." Indeed, all of it is true. I am no psychologist, educator, or child development expert. I have three children, but we are a mixed family. It is only Jupiter, the youngest one, I am raising from scratch. My two older children were brought up by their birth mother until she passed away when they were in their early teens. I cannot claim to be a parenting expert.

Birth of the Idea

So, who am I to write about a parenting approach? What qualifies me to write about a tool to train children? My mother is child development psychologist, but that does not make me one. I am a mom, a parent. I love my children and want the best life has to offer for them. I am organized, disciplined, and constantly looking for better ways to accomplish my tasks. I have a tremendous desire for simplicity, and even a greater passion for doing the best I can with all I do. I want to make a difference, to make the world a better place. The honest truth is that while I have a good education my qualification to write about parenting comes from having done it, form discovering this miracle and practicing and refining it over many years. My qualification is that I invented something that works.

It does not serve anyone to keep my idea to myself. Why should I shrink and hold back simply because I do not have a degree in child development? There are plenty of books about how to raise children by child development experts. This one is by an accomplished engineer who went to Harvard Business School and came up with a way to use that education and her personality to apply an old method to a new situation. However, history demonstrates that innovation often comes from a non-expert that can think outside the box. What about you, do *you* want to try it?

3.   Proposal to Change the Game

I suggest you challenge your usual method of training up your children

Traditionally we have taught children by instructing them. This is called the didactic method. We teach them what to do and what not to do, or show them how to do something.

On the other hand, the case method teaches by inquiry and questioning. It is also called the Socratic Method for the Greek philosopher Socrates who gained notoriety using a similar approach 2,500 years ago. Customarily, the case method has been used with adult students. The Socratic teacher does not instruct but rather asks the students questions to help them discover the solutions themselves. The idea is that the student, by seeking answers to questions, acquires the desired knowledge and gains a deeper understanding of the issues at hand.

I suggest to change the game in parenting a bit, and move from the didactic method of teaching and instruction to the Socratic method of inquiry and engagement. I am not proposing to stop teaching and instructing our children, but rather to start using the case method as an alternative when there is an opportunity. I am not pushing you to replace your parenting strategies with the case method, but to use it to complement and build on what you are already doing.

Typically you tell your child what to do and then establish systems so you can enforce those behaviors

Let me explore this concept a little further. According to the traditional premise, when we teach or correct our children, we point to the specific behaviors we want changed and establish punishments or rewards. For example, the child has left his toys on the floor after you have specifically told him to put them back where they belong. You may say repeatedly, "Please pick up your toys." Perhaps you threaten to take the toys away if it happens again or punish the child with isolation after too many offenses. The isolation punishment could be a time-out, thinking-time, or sitting alone with hands on his lap. You point to the wrong, explain what the child should do, and then establish consequences to affirm the desired behavior.

This is a concept that makes sense and works pretty well. The child is learning how he is expected to behave and is punished by the parents when he does wrong. However, this approach may have a bad effect on your child's self-esteem.

Another tactic is to give rewards for the desired behaviors. One of my friends uses a reward system where her daughters get stickers to add to their charts every time they do a chore for which they are responsible. Once either one of the girls reaches a certain number of stickers, she gets a prize. The girls love it, and it works for them. In another family, the father has established a dinner rule. The children will get a little bit of each dinner dish on their plates. Once the child has finished everything on his plate, he can have more of whatever he wants. It works for them. The children are learning at least to try various dishes. The idea is that the parents tell the children what to do and establish systems to enforce those behaviors. However, this type of rewards-based system may also have unintended damaging effects.

The case method ushers your child to discover the right thing to do, then self-monitor and assume responsibility for his choices

Using the case method in its most elementary form fundamentally changes this concept. You move from telling your child what to do to helping him decide for himself, starting with the simplest tasks. I have tried it and seen it work. It is a game changer. Your child thinks about the case dilemma and then acts—so it looks like magic to you, for you do not see the changes inside his mind. Later, you see your child do something you want him to do without having asked him. It is as if he magically took ownership of his actions, without any additional oversight from you.

Something powerful happens when your child imagines through a scenario and then positions to make a judgment for another child, the case protagonist, instead of himself. Your child becomes the one who decides right from wrong, or wise from unwise. Your child becomes the ruler for the protagonist. Most important, after a case is repeated a few times, your child starts to *own* the wise course of action. This is the magic. When your child then faces a similar situation in his life, his brain and heart are already prepped for the wise course of action. Increasingly, he resolves to make a wise decision in his own reality.

Your child then fathers the man he becomes. He learns to consider and take responsibility for his actions early in his life. What we learn as young children has a powerful impact on whom we become as adults. We carry those attitudes, outlooks, and how to respond to life situations with us into our adult lives.

4. Anyone Can Do It

You do not have to be a Harvard graduate to use the case method

In this chapter I show why anyone can do it. I pull together some of the whys that make the approach so compelling. The case method is simple and easy, flexible, universal to any value system, age-independent, and proven.

As I shared earlier, I began trying the case method approach with Jupiter, my son. I kept going with it, because Jupiter loved engaging in the wise and unwise decision stories, and because I saw how well the method worked. I told others about it. Some of them tried it. We talked about it. Some of them thought it was too much, while others were having fun with the process. I listened to them. I gained some diverse perspectives from parents and other caregivers, nannies and grandparents. Even with the pushbacks, the case method was a winner. It was not a surprise, for the method itself was proven long before I came along to extrapolate and take it to use with children.

The method is simple and easy to do

Describing simple life scenarios, cases, is so much easier than coming up with imaginary tales. When I create a story about the Silly Elephant and Sunny Bunny, Jupiter's favorite creatures, I have to come up with a setup in a fun place, something silly for the Silly Elephant to do, and then how the two, Silly Elephant and Sunny Bunny, play through the story. It is not something I can always come up with on the fly. To pull it off, usually I would have to be in a relaxed setting without distractions.

The case scenarios are not like that. Or at least we should not make them so complicated. Anyone can describe an everyday life experience in its most basic form. You must not make it harder than it is. If you make it too complicated, it leads to fatigue. It drains enthusiasm from both you and your child and becomes unworthy of the time spent.

Melanie, one of my friends, tried the case approach for a while and then stopped because it was too much work. I asked her what she was doing. She shared a case story with me. It was impressive, storybook material for sure. With her eloquence, Melanie had made an everyday situation with her daughter sound like a magic fairy tale from the Hans Christian Andersen fables. There was a moral to the story, just like those famous fables. However, the case method—as I have defined it—is distinct from elaborate stories with moral lessons. Such stories may have their place, but are not to be confused with the case method approach I am explaining.

The cases are simple. Melanie had taken a simple event and decorated it. She'd made a masterpiece when all she needed was an uncomplicated illustration. What Melanie did was not necessary. In fact, it may distract from the issue to be addressed. The advantage of the case method is its simplicity. Anyone can describe a life event, but not everyone is a master storyteller. Fortunately, you don't have to be.

The case stories are so simple that when I write them down, it is almost embarrassing. Nevertheless it is what makes them work with children, and easy for parents to employ. When I started writing down some example cases for the case example section of this book, I was tempted to color and decorate them. They sounded so plain. There was nothing to them. Yet that was the point. It was what had worked the best, to stay focused on the issue at hand and the event from the child's perspective. This is a major benefit of the case method approach, the simplicity and ease with which anyone can tell a case story to his child.

No background or embellishment is needed to make a point. What's more, any such overdoing will only distract from the key idea. The simpler the better, for the purpose of these conversations is not to build vocabulary, but rather to engage the child's mind and imagination.

Just keep it simple!

The approach is flexible

If you decide to try the case method approach, you do not have to replace your other parenting strategies with it. I talked about this earlier. The case method is not an all-or-nothing type of practice. You can apply it to complement what you are already doing, or test it when other systems have not worked. You do not have to tell a case story every day for it to start working its miracle. There is no threshold number to reach or a frequency to achieve.

For example, when I first realized how well the case approach was working with Jupiter, we cuddled on the sofa and did wise and unwise decisions almost every day. Jupiter was loving it and asking me to cuddle with him and tell the decision stories. It was our daily special time. However, after some weeks of it I needed a break. We halted the case stories for a few weeks. Even then I kept spotting case story opportunities while playing with my son or watching him with other children. I would recall the events later in the evening when I was putting my son to bed.

We re-engaged with the case stories. I would call to mind an approximation of what had happened earlier that day, bring it up disguised in a case scenario with a little boy making a wise or unwise decision. Then I asked Jupiter what he thought of the decision the little boy made. I started asking some follow-up questions about the decision. Jupiter was more engaged than simply recognizing a wise or unwise decision. It gave us a chance to reflect on what had happened earlier in the day. I did not do it every day, maybe once or twice a week. Every day, once a week, once a month, or whenever, it is up to you.

In the end, effecting the case method is more art than science. Though I describe selected rules of thumb later in this book, they are not rigid. They are my best attempt to explain what makes the case method successful in parenting children. I believe there may be as many ways of employing the case method as there are parents, some with small and others with big variations from the way I implemented it. You can adjust it to fit your preferences, style, and family routines.

The flexibility using the case method is well illustrated in business education at our finest universities. They take advantage of the Socratic Method to varying degrees. For example, at Harvard Business School they teach exclusively with the case method. Mark, my husband, received his business degree from University of Canterbury in Christchurch, New Zealand, and they taught marketing exclusively by the case method. On the other hand, at other superb business programs such as at the University of Chicago, they rely mostly on lectures to teach the fundamentals of business, only mixing in cases occasionally. Similarly, you do not have to go all in to get some of the benefits—you can do it the Harvard way or the Chicago way.

You do not have to faithfully follow the process to a letter. Rather, try it, push yourself a little, and see how it works for you and how much of it you are comfortable with.

The method applies universally to any child and any value system

You do not have to be a Harvard graduate, nor your child Harvard bound, to use the case method. But your child might become Harvard bound after you use the case method for a few years! If you love your child and can describe an event in your own words, you qualify. The beauty of the case method approach is that anyone can do it and any child can benefit from it. We can impact the world for wisdom, one child—our own—at a time.

The measurable intelligence level of your child does not matter. You are not teaching business decisions with complex data or academics. You are using cases to help your child own wise decision-making. Ability to imagine a described scenario is the only skill required from your child. The way I propose to use the case method applies to all children, because every child can visualize events described to them. Children around the world love stories. The case method is merely another way to tell a story.

Neither is the case method tied to a particular religious or moral system. It is not a prescription to teach a restricted cultural set of values. Parents or caregivers can use the case stories to apply any value system to a child's life. You will see this when you read through the case story examples in Section III. You will see a range of morality expressed in the case stories. You may agree with some of them, yet not with the others. But of course they are just illustrations, not suggestions of what you should teach.

Flexibility is the beauty of the approach. Remember, the case stories in this book are from my experiences with Jupiter and some of my friends' experiences with their children. You will create and share your own simple stories with your child from your everyday life. No matter what your beliefs, the approach allows your child to develop his own inner compass, guided by your values.

The case method can benefit children of all ages

I focus on young—preschool and elementary age—children in this book. But this is only one example of the application of the case method. I believe the case method is as comprehensive as any teaching system I've seen in any age group.

I have no doubt we can adapt the case method to accommodate the other age groups. If you share some case story examples from this book with your child who is older than elementary school age, he might find most of them a bit naive. He has his own issues. The case stories for his age group would need to be modified to be a little more complex and nuanced, dealing with his everyday issues. Children mature as they approach the teenage years, and as teenagers they face decisions that have long-lasting implications, so they present a whole new set of dilemmas. Yet their decisions can—maybe more than the little one's decisions about sharing a toy—have long-lasting consequences.

I was recently at a wedding party, and someone asked about my book. I shared the big idea and gave some examples. A lively discussion ensued. One of the ladies said, "How would you do this with teenagers? I have a sticky situation. My son was invited to a party. He asked me if he could go. I asked him about the party, and he said it was at somebody's house. One of the parents would probably be there. Most of the class was invited. I asked him if there was going to be drinking, and he said he would think so, but he was not sure." She looked at me. I did not know what to say.

She continued, "The issue is that I know—and my son knows—that there is going to be drinking and hooking up. But how do I talk to him about it? I do not want to tell him what to do, nor do I want him to get in trouble. How would you do the case method in this situation?" I was speechless at first. Initially, I thought she should tell her son about her own experience and what she had done, but then I realized that was probably the last approach she should take.

"How would you approach a situation like that with the case method?" she asked again.

I paused, "Well, how could we do a case scenario about a party like that?" I continued, "Maybe the case story could be a likely scenario from a party? Let's just imagine what could take place."

I suggested she take her son aside and describe a scenario to him. The key would be to be specific about the party, the music, the dancing, the drinking, the girls, and the boys. She could describe a hookup scenario. She could picture in detail what he would see, then lay out the decision to make. What would he do? In a scenario like this, the mother could also proceed to tell what the young man in the case chose to do and what the consequences were. Perhaps he had to pay child support for the next eighteen years of his life. Perhaps he caught an infection requiring regular treatment, or worse, one that was incurable.

We laughed about it at the wedding party. What struck me as I was driving home was that the case method was potent with teenagers, perhaps *especially* with teenagers. But that it is also a bit different. A parent is often considering granting permission to a teenager who seeks freedom to do something that requires a parent's approval. A case story is not the way to give permission—whether or not the lady's teenage boy could go to the party—but a way to help a teenager think about how he will, or should, act in a given situation. Permission should be given clearly as yes, or no, or yes under certain circumstances such as if homework is finished, or if parents are supervising. But, after permission is granted, the case method could be very valuable in guiding the teenager to act wisely, with consideration, rather than just on impulse or following what others are doing. Yet clearly, use of the method with teenagers requires modification and a different, more sophisticated (and maybe salacious!) story.

The case method is tried and true
As I pointed out earlier, Socrates used the case dialogue 2,500 years ago, and Harvard Business School has risen to world-wide dominance using the case method. However, there are as many definitions of the case method today as there are applications. The way the case method is applied at Harvard Business School and at law schools is a far cry from the way Socrates used it. Yet the approach continually has been referred to as the case method over these 2,500 years.

Socrates nurtured his students, gently asking questions that deconstructed the students' ideas about the most basic definitions of virtue. Socrates only wanted short answers to his exact points. The students would eventually, via their dialogue with Socrates, discard their old ideas and dig deeper into the matters under study. The end result was an increased understanding.

But the case method at law and business schools is rather different. The process is not deconstructive, but constructive. The students construct, or pull together, from the large amount of detailed case information via the case discussion in class. The teacher questions and leads the debate to direct the students to a certain way of thinking or certain required knowledge. Socrates's case discussions were void of the intense—even contentious—questioning often present at modern professional schools. All derivations of the case method work, attesting to the potency of the approach.

In my version of the case method, we adopt a hybrid. We embrace Socrates's nurturing tenderness and focus on short answers. We also go with Socrates in that there is no need for reams of data analysis on the part of the student. We fold in from the business school approach the teacher's role to provide a story that is the basis for consideration, and then lead the student into a certain way of thinking or knowledge. We do not leave the student hanging, not knowing whether he knew a solution or not. This crossbreed appears to share the power of both approaches.

I wonder if and how Socrates applied the method of teaching with inquiry with his own three children. Maybe he did what I am proposing in this book?

5.   What's in It for You

It pays off for you and your child to try the case method

You may wonder why you should bother. Why change the way you do things? Why go to the effort? Is it really worth it? I dare say the direct benefits to you and your child far outweigh the little extra energy it takes to try it.

When you start using the case method, you bond with your child, gain confidence and respect as a parent, and experience less drama with everyday conflicts. By engaging in the case discussions your child builds self-reliance and grit, improves his literacy skills, and gains the strength of character he needs to make wise decisions later in life, whether online or offline.

You bond with your child

We bond with someone when we spend time with them. We bond with our children when we experience life together, teach and learn. Engaging in the case stories is an opportunity to connect.

Involving your child with storytelling is also a way to express your love to him. In his heart, "I tell you a story" equates to "I care about you." I have yet to meet a child who does not love stories, especially when a parent tells their own story. It endears us to our children when we put ourselves out there and dare to do something new and creative with them. Furthermore, rewarding your child with an expression of love, say a hug or a tickle, when he answers the case wisely, is an expression of physical affection and closeness for which he yearns.

I know when Jupiter comes to me and asks if we can do wise and unwise decision stories, he not only longs for the stories but wants to be with me, to engage in *our way* of talking about wise and unwise decisions, or good and bad manners. It has brought us closer, fortified our bond, and strengthened our love for each other. As a parent I naturally make mistakes, but love overcomes them.

You gain confidence as a parent

Many parents consider it important to instill self-confidence in their children. Most of the parenting literature focuses on what you need to do to assure your child is building confidence. I would like to turn it around. What about *your* confidence as a parent? What role do you think it plays in raising confident children? Perhaps we should work on our own self-confidence, too?

Increased confidence in my parenting skills has been an unexpected benefit from practicing the case method. As a parent, I have appreciated that by engaging Jupiter in the case method process I have gained certainty about the way I train him. In turn, my trust in what I am doing as a parent directly emboldens Jupiter. I act confidently when I pull away from a bad situation only to address it later. I look patient and self-controlled even when I may not be. Jupiter observes and appreciates it.

Your child views a confident parent with more trust, respect, and love. It makes you more effective as a parent. It also feels safe for your child to be around you when you act with assurance. If you constantly fluctuate between knowing what to do and flying by the seat of your pants, you do not instill confidence in your child. The way to raise confident children is to be a confident parent. Participating in the case stories with your children accomplishes this.

Telling a case story helps your child save face

None of us likes being publicly humiliated or interrogated by an authority or our spouse. The same applies to your child. He does not appreciate being reprimanded and told about his wrongdoings in front of his friends or other adults. In fact, it appears that children who get constantly corrected in front of their friends make it a self-fulfilling prophesy. They misbehave as if they are expected to act that way, do wrong at every turn. After a while, misbehavior is ingrained.

On the other hand, when you save face for your child, he is grateful you did not confront the situation in front of others. It communicates trust, love, and respect for his feelings. Better to wait until you are removed from the situation and then, in a calm, private setting address the wrongdoing one-on-one with a case story.

Emily and Sean had a five-year-old daughter, Margaret, and a baby boy, Matthew. They had been invited to dinner at a restaurant with David, Sean's colleague from work. Unfortunately, their babysitter had a last-minute emergency and was not able to make it. Instead of canceling, or Emily staying at home with the children, they decided to take the children with them. The children were used to eating out, and Emily and Sean did not expect any major problems.

But, when Margaret received her meal, she made a face. Something was obviously wrong with her plate. Abruptly, she pushed it away from her, "I did not order this!" The plate hit her glass of milk and tipped it over. The milk poured down the side of the table. Most of the milk landed on David's lap.

Sean and Emily were quick to apologize for Margaret, who did not say anything at first. After a moment, she repeated she had not ordered French fries. The parents were upset with Margaret. It was clearly not an accident. However, instead of making a scene, they helped clean up. Emily asked Margaret about the order, and the waiter took care of it.

At home that evening, Sean put Margaret to bed while Emily took care of the baby. He was proud of himself for not blowing up at the restaurant. Yet he wanted to address it. Sean said, "Margaret, may I tell you a story?"

"Once there was a little girl, her name was Leia. Leia was a princess. One day a king from a faraway land arrived to have dinner with Princess Leia's family. The king and the queen, Leia's parents, received the foreign king in the palace dining hall. It was a beautiful evening. Princess Leia requested her favorite meal, rice with grilled chicken. Her mother and father were talking with the visiting king. When the meals came, Princess Leia noticed she did not have the right dish. Instead of what she had ordered, Princess Leia had received a steak and a baked potato. She was taken aback. She did not like it.

She looked up to her mother, the queen. "Excuse me, mother," Leia said.

Her mother turned to her. "Yes, Leia?"

Leia continued, "It looks like there has been a mistake. I ordered chicken with rice. Do you think it would be all right to let the waiter know?"

Sean stopped. He smiled and looked at Margaret. "Margaret, what do think about that? Do you think Princess Leia made a wise decision to address the situation in that manner?"

In this example the father, Sean, helped his daughter, Margaret, save face at the restaurant by not making a scene when the incident happened. He addressed the situation afterward, in private with Margaret, by recounting a case story with a case protagonist his daughter would admire. The case protagonist behaved admirably. Margaret knew it was the wise decision. She wanted to be like Princess Leia who was one of her heroines. Margaret knew she had not behaved that way herself. The way she had acted had been unwise. With that, Sean let it go. Margaret made that connection herself. Sean did not point the finger; he trusted Margaret to evaluate her own behavior.

Another way to help your child save face is to prepare him for potentially embarrassing situations ahead of time. Your child can learn by observing the case protagonist's failure before falling short himself.

One of my friends, Caroline, had a daughter who was not wiping her rear-end properly after using the bathroom. The father, instead of nagging her about it, chose to tell her a story about a little girl, Elena, who did not wipe her bottom properly. In the case story, Elena had gone to school where the other children had started smelling it in the classroom while they all sat on the mat. The teacher had smelled it, too, and proceeded to have everyone go to the restroom to make sure they were clean. Elena had gone, but she had turned red when she came back to the class. Everyone knew it was she. There was no need for any reminders after the graphic illustration. Often father knows best.

You can manage with less drama to get a point across

Imagine the following: your daughter has just learned to ride her bicycle but she does not like wearing a helmet. You keep telling her to put her helmet on every time you ride at the park. She never seems to put it on herself. You are constantly reminding her, sometimes frustrated, "Please put your helmet on!" You tell her she can get hurt if she does not have her helmet on. But it is not helping. You have to keep nagging if you want to make sure the helmet goes on before she rides her bike.

What would the case method alternative suggest?

Imagine the following: Your daughter has just learned how to ride the bicycle, and you have come to a park to ride and play. You pull your daughter aside and sit down on the park bench. "Before we go, I want you to listen to me. Can I tell you a story? It is about a little girl your age. Her name was Kaitlyn. Kaitlyn loved riding her bicycle. She had been riding her bicycle for a year. She did not fall down any more. She had good balance. One afternoon she wanted to go ride her bike with her friend Sarah. She asked her mother if she could go, just for a short ride in the neighborhood. Her mother said, 'Yes.' Kaitlyn put on her shoes and ran off to get her bicycle. The helmet was hanging on the handlebar. Kaitlyn stopped. She did not want to wear it. She was only going to ride in the neighborhood. She left the helmet and rode off with her bicycle. Sarah was waiting for Kaitlyn in front of her house. They rode off. They were having a good time. All of a sudden, Kaitlyn hit a pine cone on the road and lost her balance. She veered towards the middle of the road. A car was behind her. The car hit Kaitlyn. She fell off her bicycle and hit her head on the road. An ambulance came and took her to the hospital."

You look at your daughter, deep in her eyes, and say, "What do you think? Did Kaitlyn make a wise or an unwise decision?" Your daughter knows the answer. Kaitlyn should have worn her helmet. Your daughter asks, "Is that a real story, or just pretend?" You are quiet for a moment and say, "It is real. It happened." You tell her the names are not the same names, but the story is real. Then you take your daughter's hand and say, "Let's go get our bikes." You say nothing to her about wearing her helmet, but let her choose to take it and put it on. When she does that with the case scenario as a backdrop, I assure it makes a powerful imprint on her brain. She is not putting on her helmet so much from you telling her to do it, but from imagining a consequence of not wearing a helmet. It is for herself she is putting it on.

The drama from nagging, confrontation, or argument can be replaced with the case story, in the prior example a rather dramatic case story. In that example, when you describe the accident and the preceding moments in detail, it makes it more real to your child. Your child thinks it is something that could actually happen. It is not pretend.

When you tell your child what to do, especially to stay safe, you have a different perspective. You know what could happen. You may have witnessed an accident or experienced one. It is not so with your child. To him the warnings are mere abstractions, they do not mean much, they are just restricting requests from an interfering parent, you. To act on them he would not be doing so out of a clear understanding of the risk, but rather from obedience. The case scenario changes this and puts your child through a potential experience. It helps him to own the wise decision to avoid a risky behavior.

Your child gains self-reliance and strength of character

Gaining self-reliance and strength of character, or grit, may be the most ensuring and far-reaching benefit of the case method approach. This is a part of the miracle.

As your child gains confidence in making wise choices for the case protagonist, he gradually gains confidence in making wise decisions on his own. As wisdom becomes more and more his guiding light, he is less vulnerable to peer pressure, bullying, or confusion. Your child starts to realize how he is in control of his decisions and responses to life, and eventually, his own destiny.

A memorable moment when the case method miracle stopped me on my tracks was when Jupiter had a grandparents' and special friends' day at school. My friend Leslie went to visit Jupiter at his school as his special friend. Leslie had frequented playgrounds with us for a couple years. Jupiter adored her.

When I asked how the visit had gone, Leslie told me about a powerful incident. The guests had gathered for a show by the children at the auditorium. After the show the children met their grandparents and special friends on the floor. A group of boys was playing and acting out about the show. Jupiter was part of the group. Leslie heard one of the boys taunting the others to do something. She was not sure what it was, but she noted Jupiter pull back a bit and tilt his head to the side, as if making an estimate of something. Then Jupiter turned around and went to Leslie. He said, "They are up to mischief. It is unwise. I am not going to do it."

It was a mighty manifestation of courage and resolve, or grit, for a five-year-old. I knew we were on a good start for building grit in other areas, too. It is easier to build self-reliance and grit in small things first, then transfer the quality to more complex issues in life. Such is how leadership of our own character development begins.

Case conversations prepare your child for literacy

Creating a dialogue with your child is as important to preparing for literacy as reading to him. In other words, to prepare for literacy, your attention should not be only on reading and vocabulary, but also on discussion. Engaging your child with short cases serves this purpose.

Having grown up in Finland and come through the Finnish school system all the way through high school, I have been intrigued by the consistent ranking of the Finnish schooling among the world's best. I have read the studies with interest, especially the research about early education years, since it applies directly to engaging Jupiter with the short case stories.

The Finnish preschool curriculum instructs that the basis for literacy during the early years comes from both listening to someone and being listened to by someone. In other words, to prepare for literacy we must engage verbally with children—and interact with them, not merely lecture them with a "Now, you listen to me!"—during their early years. Just teaching the ABCs and reading to them is not sufficient.

Who would have thought that the way you lead your child to do right and shun wrong, the *way* you do it, can improve his literacy skills later in life.

Wise decisions offline translate to wise decisions online

Initially your child interacts with the digital world mostly via electronic games and educational applications. He does not have to make decisions about social media, nor does he use the internet for school work. You tend to control the time he spends with electronic media.

Once your child, as a tween or a teen, gets access to his own smartphone and the internet, the openings for unwise decisions and intellectual dumbing down are abundant. For example, digital media increases opportunities to be distracted from face-to-face conversations and from getting homework—or any other work—completed. Peer pressure and the desire to be popular extend to the digital realm. Many teens calculate their self-worth from likes, shares, and retweets.

Research regarding teens' online behavior has found that wise decision-making in real life translates into online behavior. This conclusion is key to understanding a key advantage of using the case method early. The case method approach is a winner in *preparing* your child to embrace the digital world to his advantage. It guides him to make wise decisions. Even if the wise-decision making is not related directly to specific dilemmas online; according to the research, it transfers to online choices.

The strength of character, or grit, developed via the case method miracle, applies to any predicament, including online behavior. Your child's transition into the digital world will be safer and less overwhelming when he has already—via the case method miracle—developed strength of character by the time he is fully and productively engaged with the internet.

In addition, the case method approach strengthens the bond between you and your child. When you have a strong relationship with your child, it is easier to navigate the challenges and exploit the learning opportunities presented by the digital world. When your child first gets online, he does not mind if you are watching and guiding him. It is easier to teach some rules of the road at that point. Later as a teenager, he is online on his own and prefers it that way. Your teen does not want you hovering over his shoulders, and you are often not even around to check. When there is a question or he has made a mistake, your teen is likely to come to you for help if he has a close relationship with you.

In summary, the case method prepares your child for what waits for him online and with social media by helping him to practice making wise decisions under a variety of circumstances, by developing inner strength, and by building a close relationship with you.

6.   How It Works

The process works when it is straightforward and predictable

To lead you to start on this process, let's look at how it could work for you. The cases you use should be short, one minute or less. You describe life situations familiar to your child, scenarios with which your child can identify immediately. The case story always ends with a question. The question is about the case protagonist, and it can take two forms. It may be about what he did, or what he should do. The process is uncomplicated, and your child should quickly learn to expect a short story and a clear question.

In the first case, the question is closed-ended. "Did the little boy make a wise choice?" The answer is a yes or no. These yes-or-no cases work best if your child is just learning to make decisions on his own, say, aged two or three. They also do well with your older child when you are showing a way to handle a situation and want your child to recognize its wisdom or foolishness.

In the second case—with an open-ended question—your child has to formulate a plan of action for the case protagonist. Your child may be more challenged and enjoy cases where the protagonist is left to *make* the decision in the end. The question you pose to your child is: "What would be the wise decision?" A simple yes or no does not suffice. However, the simplicity of the case situation, your child's innate ability to relate to it, the joy in discovering the answer, and the reward of your approval make the process fun and uncomplicated.

Use your judgment and knowing your child to decide on a case by case basis whether to use a closed-ended question or an open-ended one. Both approaches work.

In both cases the teaching idea is to affirm the behaviors you approve and desire for your child. Your child learns not only that a dilemma calls for a decision, but that not all decisions are equal—just making any decision isn't good enough. Rather, the best decision is the wise one. Your child starts to think about consequences, cause and effect, but in a very simple way.

Relevant and simple scenarios speak directly to your child

There are two principles to guide your story making: relevance and simplicity.

Your one-on-one engaging with your child and the relevance of the cases make the cases up-close and personal. You describe the case about a little boy facing a dilemma your child has either recently faced or will likely encounter in the near future. Your child instinctively puts himself into the role of the protagonist when you ask whether the little boy in the story made a wise or unwise decision or what the little boy in the case should do. This involves your child's imagination, and you cannot expect your child to imagine something with which he is unfamiliar, or something which is not a part of his world.

In addition to making them relevant, it is important to keep your cases simple. This way your child will experience joy—instead of frustration—in discovering his answer. You must clutch it in your heart that the case method for your child is not a test or a brain exercise, but a technique to usher him onto the path of wise decision-making and self-reliance. You start out with smaller and simpler rather than small and simple. You start with small steps so your child discovers success and joy in knowing the wise answer. Once answering becomes a positive experience for your child, he starts to desire more of that feeling without consciously striving for it. I have observed that the desire for "I know how to do it!" resides in every child's DNA.

Steering away from finger-pointing pushes for accountability

The central idea of the case method approach is to push for your child to take responsibility for his actions, not to teach him to point fingers and compare himself with his siblings or friends. This is a delicate matter.

I have witnessed many a friend to walk into the comparison trap without noticing it. I have walked into it and still not aware of having done so. Rather than trying to explain this in theory, let me illustrate with an example where you can see how to avoid raising a finger-pointer.

Say Jupiter and I observe his friend using foul language and playing rough at the pool. Jupiter and I notice. We look at each other. It confirms to me that Jupiter has witnessed his friend's improper behavior.

Later if I decide to make a case story about a little boy doing the bad behavior like Jupiter's friend did, I am treading on dangerous waters. Jupiter would now shift to focus on how his friends are behaving and what they are doing instead of what he is doing and how he is choosing to behave.

To avoid this, I could choose one of at least two options. First, I could let enough time pass, say weeks, before making the scenario into a case story, thus minimizing the association with Jupiter's friend. If Jupiter recalls the event and makes a reference to his friend having done that, I could still recover by redirecting. I could say, "You are right, Jupiter, but what about you? What would you do in that situation?"

Second, I could retell the scenario but change it to be about choosing wisely. The case would be about a little boy going to the pool with his friend and being excited about playing. The little boy would hear some other boys using bad language, yelling, and playing rough. But this little boy would choose wisely and not go along. Now the case would be about Jupiter, affirming his choice to keep his good manners even when others are misbehaving.

If Jupiter follows up with a finger-pointing comment after I have told Jupiter a case, I pause and address the issue. It is simple to do by asking him what he would do. "What about you, Jupiter? What would *you* do?" My role as the case storyteller is to help Jupiter focus on owning the responsibility of not pointing fingers at others.

The process derails without rewards

After your child answers the case question, you have an opportunity to reward him. Rewards that express love for your child are an essential part of the process. They can be hugs, cuddles, praise, stickers, or whatever your child appreciates the most. They are the seal for mutual bonding. The rewards give the case stories the momentum.

If your child answers correctly, you reward him. The idea is to have the cases so clear-cut and relevant your child has no difficulty in identifying whether the choice the child in the case made was wise or unwise. If your child does not answer correctly, you can adjust the story to make the wise choice more obvious, or you can discuss the dilemma with the child.

Let me illustrate how the process might derail if you ignore the rewards. My friend Jane set out to try the case method with her daughters, Tina and Kelly. When I checked with Jane a couple weeks later, she was defeated. After her third case story, the girls had not wanted to hear them anymore. Jane gave details on the cases she had told Tina and Kelly. They seemed relevant and simple. We wondered what the problem could be, and realized she had not used any rewards in the end. The rewards make it fun and keep the energy up.

Constantly bringing up the negative kills any chances of success

We uncovered another issue with the cases Jane had used. Each case Jane had told the girls was a rehashing of an event where the girls, or one of them, had behaved badly.

Clearly, Tina and Kelly had come to view the cases stories as a way for the mother to point a finger to their wrongdoings. What Jane had intended to be a positive, encouraging bonding experience, had turned into repeated reminders about the mother's disapproval.

We discussed possible solutions. Jane decided to leave the cases for a while and then re-introduce them. Only this time she would describe positive experiences and shower the girls with stickers to help launch the process. It worked.

Knowing your family dynamics helps you to tailor the process

Jane's experience doing cases with Tina and Kelly highlighted another important variable you should keep in mind. The case method works best when you use it with the right frequency and timing for *your* child.

Depending on your child and the dynamic he has with you or the caregiver, the optimal frequency of telling cases varies. The case method works when the experience is desirable and interesting, when you lead the storytelling at the most teachable moments. Different children have different teachable moments as you well may know. Jupiter, my son, might love the couch cuddles the best, but your child may be in the mood for wise and unwise decisions while he is talking about his school day. It requires that you observe and get to know your child enough so you recognize these personal opportunities. It is a delicate experiment of trial and error to figure the right timing and balance, for your child.

When the case stories are relevant and simple, and the frequency is suitable, the momentum starts to build. What seems to take place is that your child begins to own the desire to strive for wise decisions. From an early age, he starts to make judgment calls about which way to go instead of blindly doing what you say. It makes him feel good about knowing the wise way even in instances where he has taken the unwise path. Your child starts to develop a self-concept;

he is separate from you and capable of making wise decisions for himself. The aspiration to make a wise choice now comes from within himself. Even if he fails next time, he is learning to evaluate his options and to take responsibility for his own actions. The momentum builds, and your child develops the all-elusive grit to pursue wise decisions for himself, on his own.

From observing Jupiter—especially those early years at two and three—it was clear to me that he mostly loved to please his daddy and me. Most children want their parents' approval, not disapproval, in public and in private. With the case stories I have been able to endorse and praise Jupiter *knowing* the wise choice even when he had done something wrong. I have been able to use the case method to shepherd my child to judge himself for doing the wrong action, while commending him for knowing the right thing to do in that situation and encouraging him to pursue a better choice next time. I thought it was brilliant. The transfer of ownership for Jupiter's behavior moved from me to him. The case stories have allowed me to take advantage of the positive learning and praising Jupiter for knowing how to make wise decisions, instead of focusing on the reprimand of the bad choices.

Modeling humility and learning as parents

Our children are more apt to watch what we do rather than listen to what we tell them to do. Where I have used the reprimand for bad choices successfully, is with myself, openly in front of Jupiter.

To facilitate learning from our bad choices, I make a point to show how I do it with Jupiter. I continue to have plenty of opportunities for this every day. I mess up. I know it, and Jupiter knows it. I am tempted to brush it off as a mistake and just forget it, but I try to face it so we can both learn from it. First, I quickly admit my wrong. Then I ask for forgiveness if it impacted Jupiter in any way. Finally, as Jupiter forgives me, I hug him. I say, "Thank you!"

I suspect engaging in this type of "Mommy makes unwise decisions, too" dialogue has helped the case method bear more fruit than I have been able to imagine. When Jupiter is given opportunities to give me grace, it is easier for him to accept it, too, and keep his mindset fertile for learning. I model to Jupiter how failing is just another way of learning.

Let me share a recent example from my experience. Jupiter was at a summer camp for the day while I was writing this book. It was his first day at an outdoor adventure camp. The children were picked up at a coffee shop parking lot in the morning and brought back at three o'clock sharp, in a school bus.

In the afternoon I lost track of time, buried in a project. Suddenly, I looked at my watch. It was 3:04pm. Eeek! I rushed out of the house and made it right before the camp leaders had said to take any unclaimed children back to the camp at 3:15pm. Jupiter was standing in the hot sun with his backpack. I ran to him.

While driving to pick him up, I had thought to tell him some lame excuse, but quickly decided to instead tell him what had happened and my role in it. I said, "Jupiter, I am so sorry I am late. Are you all right? Have you been waiting for a long time?" Jupiter said he was all right, but it had been a long time.

I continued, "Were you afraid?"

Jupiter smiled, "Mommy, I thought you had forgotten about me."

What agony, I felt for him, and proceeded to tell him the entire situation, "Jupiter, I am so sorry. Please, I would never forget you. But this is my fault. I am late because I lost track of time. I was working on my wise and unwise decisions book. I was so focused that I forgot to look at the time. When I did, it was 3:04pm! I screamed like this, 'Eeek,' and ran out the house. I was not paying attention to what I should have, to pick you up on time. Can you please forgive me, Jupiter?"

"I can forgive you, Mommy," Jupiter said.

I hugged my sweaty, tired son, "Thank you, Sweet Love." I then asked him what he thinks I should do so I will not do this again. Jupiter solved it. I set an alarm for the rest of the week to go off when it was time to wrap up my work and get him.

The case method works with children because they love stories, can focus on simple and short ideas, love knowing the answer, and desire to be loved. It helps the cause when you can show with your own example how learning is partly about making mistakes and unwise decisions. You create a grace-filled atmosphere fertile to learning.

Easy does it, trust your gut
The best part about the case method is that it is flexible, not some all-in or nothing approach. You do not have to be telling your child cases all the time, every day, and about every event. You do not have to be on a relentless prowl for case scenarios. Easy does it.

As you read through this book it may appear that I am constantly engaging my son with the case stories, as if it is all I do. It is not the reality. It is something we do one-on-one when the opportunity is open. There have been periods when we cuddle on the sofa every day for weeks to do "wise and unwise decisions." Or there was a phase when I told Jupiter case scenarios every night before he went to bed.

However, these are the exceptions, not the rule. When Jupiter was preschool age, the more common reality in our family was a couple case stories a week. These days sometimes we go for months and forget the case stories. I do not think an everyday application is required for the case method miracle to materialize. Applying the case method with your child is a tool to add to your kit. It does not have to be an all-encompassing parenting approach, though I am sure you can make it so if you so desire. If this method does not serve you, then try something else. Or better, take this tool, change it, and make it work for you in ways I could not.

In summary, when you share relevant, short, clear, and simple cases your child develops self-reliance and strength of character. This is heightened more when you selflessly admit your own failures and discuss whether what you did was a wise or unwise decision. When rewards are given, you and your child engage and bond. Everyone wins.

7.   When and Where to Do It

We jump in, learn by trial and error, and keep it simple

The way we do it is more like trial and error than a systematic implementation of a detailed methodology. Reading this book may give you the impression that I set out to do this with Jupiter often and at prescribed occasions. It has not been like that. The process has evolved over time.

As I shared earlier, I started trying the case method stories when Jupiter was approaching three years of age. We jumped in and tried a few. There were weeks when I told Jupiter case stories about a little boy every afternoon; however, a few times a week was more the norm. Then there were periods when a month went by without case stories.

I have implemented the cases with Jupiter one-on-one, except in some instances when I have shared a case story with a couple of his friends present. I have learned that the dynamic changes with several children engaging with the story. The interaction of the children among each other becomes a complicating factor. I find it easier to establish a connection when I can pay attention to one child, one issue, one reward, and one feedback loop. It also avoids the comparison trap for my child. Keeping it simple is important!

Several friends kept coming to me with questions about how I segued into the case stories and in what kind of situations I told them to Jupiter. In other words, how did I do it with him? While I was in the moment, it was usually a matter of recognizing an opening to tell a case story and taking advantage of it immediately or creating a setting to share a story. In retrospect, I see that I have used the most usual story-telling surroundings.

I have implemented wise and unwise decision cases with Jupiter in at least five settings. I coined them the couch cuddle, the car chat, the table talk, the bedtime stories, and the just-in-time. In this chapter I describe how I usually do it in each of the five settings, trusting it will help you try it your way with your child and then find your own favorite place or time to tell case stories.

We cuddle on the couch

The couch cuddle has been our favorite. It is how our process of doing wise and unwise decision cases started. Small children love cuddling with parents. When Jupiter was a toddler we would often lie on the couch. I would tell him my own stories. They were not wise and unwise case stories, but tales I came up with on the fly. Jupiter loved silly stories, so we created a character, Silly Elephant, who ended up in funny situations because he was silly.

After I made the connection between the case method at Harvard Business School and my child-rearing at home, I started mixing my stories with the cases. I would start with, "Once there was a little boy." When I ended the case story with the question of whether the little boy made a wise or unwise decision, Jupiter would smile and answer either, "Wise," or "Unwise." I would tickle him for the correct answer. He loved it and could not get enough of this kind of engagement. Just learning to speak, Jupiter would come to me and ask, "Mommy, can we do wise and unwise decisions?" Of course, cuddling on the couch was part of the request. Cuddling on the sofa with your child might be a wonderful way to start your case stories, too!

Occasionally, especially in the beginning, Jupiter would purposefully choose the wrong answer. He would tell me the little boy made a wise choice when he did something wrong, and an unwise choice when he did something well. There are several ways to handle this type of response. Mostly, I responded in kind, silliness, but no tickles or hugs. Jupiter got the message. It was funny when Jupiter said wise was unwise and unwise was wise, but he loved the tickles and the hugs and the chasing enough to mostly answer correctly.

Jupiter never seemed to truly not know, or truly get the answer wrong—he always intuitively knew the difference between wise and unwise. I did not make a big deal out of the silly answers. It has not become a habit, but he still sometimes does it. Maybe to lighten up the situation or just to have fun with it. It is all right, I make a funny face back to him.

In the sofa scenario, I have used all kinds of cases. I have described situations that took place earlier that day or the day before, events at home or elsewhere, or setups I expected Jupiter to face at school or while playing with his friends. During the couch cuddles I have also retold events I witnessed another child experience, reiterating a wise choice or re-condemning an unwise move for my son to imagine through.

In all of the couch cuddle cases Jupiter has been learning the path of wisdom while being held close to me. It became a special time for us to come together in learning about life as he saw it.

While driving I bring up recent events disguised as case stories

The second setting is what I have coined the car chat. While in the car I address recent situations where Jupiter had made either a wise or an unwise decision. I do it by taking what Jupiter had chosen to do and making it a quick case story about a little boy. The little boy in the case does not have to do what Jupiter had done but maybe I reverse it to make it the opposite. For example, if Jupiter had done something wrong, I could turn it around and show the little boy making a right choice. Then I can praise Jupiter "for knowing the wise choice" and leave it at that.

In my opinion these car chats are powerful teachable moments. A teachable moment is an unplanned opportunity when your child is ideally responsive to learning an insight. As you hop in the car, your child is captive audience without you directly staring down at him. He is physically restrained and stilled, encouraging a contemplative mood.

These opportunities in the car often rise from earlier-in-the-day episodes at a grocery store, at a playground, or at school. Maybe Jupiter had kept begging for a particular kind of candy at the grocery store, knowing we do not eat candies but on Saturdays. While not making it a big deal, I may have repeatedly responded to Jupiter, "No, we are not buying candies today. It is not candy day." But once in the car driving home, I may have told Jupiter about a little boy in the grocery store. How I do it is that I try to put myself in Jupiter's shoes, walking through the aisles in the grocery store, seeing the many interesting items, being hungry, and then finally seeing all the best candies in front of the cashier's. Then I describe that scenario as if a little boy is in it, wanting to have this and that, but not asking for it, because he knows what his mother will say. It is hard for the little boy, but he holds his mouth shut. In this case I have chosen to retell the event from the positive perspective, showing Jupiter he knows the wise way to go and praising that wise choice.

What I have to watch out with the car chats is that they do not become a constant tactic to reprimand bad behavior. It is so easy to notice when Jupiter does something wrong and then bring it up in the car. I often do not even notice the many situations where Jupiter had an opportunity to choose poorly, but instead he chose wisely. Watch out and try to catch your child doing something right!

We talk about case scenarios while having lunch or dinner

The third setting where we have applied the case method is during lunch and dinner conversations. I call them the table talks. I enjoy a snack or a lunch with Jupiter in the afternoons while Mark joins us at dinner.

In the afternoons I engage Jupiter about his morning at school or preschool, or our plans for the rest of the day. At times my little fellow chooses to discuss other topics. There are many kinds of case stories that work well when we sit around a table. What I have often done is to relate a case story to our topic at hand. Say Jupiter is telling me something about lunchroom at school. We discuss it, and then I use the opportunity and expand into case stories about a little boy in the lunch room making decisions this way and that way.

I have also used the table talk setting to tell cases about general principles such as how to obey, how to talk with grown-ups, how to behave when visiting a friend's house, how to be a host, among others. Such cases open the topic to further conversation.

At dinner I occasionally tell cases about a little boy, pointing out some bad or good table manners, one or a few at a time. It is interesting how the bad table manners sound inexcusable in a case story, yet we sometimes make those decisions. I know I am sometimes guilty of reaching out for a dish, interrupting, even chewing food with mouth open. Sharing wise and unwise decisions I have made helps Jupiter understand that learning to make wise decisions is a lifelong quest. For example, when I catch myself talking with food in my mouth, I make a point of it. "Excuse me, what was I doing? I was talking with food in my mouth. Was that a wise decision?" It also helps to bring home the point how we make choices all the time, wise and unwise, some significant and some less significant. I think it helps to keep the dinner conversations pleasant if I avoid blaming or bringing up something specific Jupiter had done wrong.

We reflect on making wise decisions at bedtime
In our family the fourth fertile setting for the case method learning is the story time before going to bed. We follow a basic bedtime routine. We clean up the play area, take a bath, brush teeth, read a few stories, and pray. In addition, I have been telling my own tales and case stories.

Creating my own narratives has shown to be valuable in many ways. First, Jupiter enjoys my simple, silly stories sometimes more than the eloquent fables in the books. Second, I have observed that Jupiter is often more engaged in my simple tales than the ones we read from books. Third, I discovered I can come up with interesting stories. It was not easy or natural at first, but I kept at it, and after a few weeks I realized that story topics were all around. Animals could talk, chairs could fly, and Jupiter's favorite, Baby Bunny, could play with him. My imaginative tales may not have been storybook material, but Jupiter loved them.

Initially I had not thought I had it in me, to come up with my own stories. Once I realized I could do it, it gave me confidence as a storyteller. The confidence I gained helped me to get going with the case stories, convincingly and with conviction. That in turn made a difference to the listener, Jupiter. I believe any parent can tell stories. We all have it in us, and it only requires a little push to get going. Children are a wonderful audience, they are so pleased with so little.

The day comes to an end at bedtime. We are naturally in a reflective mode. As long as Jupiter is not exhausted, it is an opportune moment to consider case stories about wise and unwise, right and wrong, or brave and gutless paths to take. If I cannot think of anything from Jupiter's immediate experience, then I can make up a case story about whatever I prefer. Remember that the case stories do not have to be something the child has experienced, they can be anything you consider relevant.

As I put Jupiter to bed, I often think about the next day or an important event coming up. It is a wonderful opportunity to tell a case story about an expected future scenario, thus helping Jupiter be mentally prepared to act wisely if and when the described scenario materializes. I might tell him about a little boy doing a great job with a "show and tell" or a little boy participating in a service project by working extra hard.

A sure winner at bedtime is for me to try to recall something Jupiter had done well that day, or an event when he surprised me with his thoughtfulness, and then I use it to create a case story. I retell the situation, only now about a little boy. Jupiter often starts beaming with delight when I then ask if the little boy in the story made a wise or unwise choice. He knows he did the right thing! It is an effective way to help anyone sleep well.

I use case stories for immediate feedback on Jupiter's choices

I call the last setting where I have used cases the just-in-time. As the name implies, this is when I want to bring home a point about a real time, recent situation. It does not matter where we are or what we are doing, the idea is to turn a teachable moment into a case story right there and then, quickly.

Usually I recognize these opportunities when Jupiter has done something improper, and I want to reprimand him. But, in my experience, Jupiter starts resisting the case stories quickly if I fault by using them to show him his wrongdoings too much. I have had to watch out for balancing praising via the cases and reprimanding via the cases.

To help Jupiter see his wrong actions from another perspective I often make the case story such that it is not exactly the same situation, even if the issue is the same.

For example, one afternoon I had just suggested to Jupiter we go for a hike, just him and I, since his friend's mother had informed us at the last minute that they could not meet us at the playground. I enjoy hiking with Jupiter, especially since it is so easy to do. We have many trails within a few minutes' drive from the house and do not need other people to do it.

Well, Jupiter did not think it was such a good idea and responded curtly, "I don't want to do that."

Since I did not think it was a nice way to respond to a suggestion, I countered, "OK. Can I tell you a quick story? You remember the little boy? One time he was at the playground with his two friends. They ran out of things to do. None of them could think of anything to do. Then the little boy had an idea. He was not sure if it was a good idea, but he thought they could consider it. He suggested they pretend the climbing equipment is an eagle's nest, and they are eagles launching off from it. One of his friends laughed, what a bad idea, he sure would not want to play *that*."

I stopped the story. I waited a few moments and asked Jupiter if he thought the friend had been kind and encouraging in the way he had responded. Did he respond wisely to the suggestion the other boy made? Jupiter knew right away that the little boy must have felt hurt the way his friend slammed his suggestion. We then talked about what kind of language we can use when someone has an idea we may not like so much. This was just in time for Jupiter to realize he had done the same thing to me when I had suggested hiking to replace the canceled playdate.

Jupiter said, "Mommy, I love you." I suspected *he* had connected the case story scenario to his own response to me. Perhaps Jupiter realized he would not want to hurt me because he loved me. I gave him a bear-big hug and said how much I loved him, too. I did not say a word about his bad behavior matching that of the little boy in the case. It had clicked, and I let it be.

When I tell the case story immediately after Jupiter's transgression, it helps to change it from the exact scenario while keeping the transgression in the story.

I use the just-in-time setting if at all possible. I find it easiest because I can recall the situation in detail. It also helps me refrain from reprimanding Jupiter in public, if—while the event is unfolding—I make a decision to do a case story about it later. It is also easier for Jupiter to make the connection. In the prior example of how I did it, Jupiter could see the impact of what he had done, the hurting of the other person. Later, he may not have. But without my ever spelling it out, because it was closely connected in time, he could see the unwise course of action immediately.

The just-in-time cases about another child in the same situation Jupiter had just experienced is a way of helping him see himself from another perspective and conclude about his behavior with his own wise and unwise criteria. It eliminates the need to blame and demoralize. I believe most children know when they have done something wrong. This approach supports them in evaluating their own conduct. Often when I share a case story immediately or shortly after an incident I change the situation a bit to avoid a direct finger-pointing. In the previous example, I used a case story where friends were sharing ideas with each other instead of a mother suggesting a plan to her son. I also turned it upside down, made it about making a wise decision and about what might have be going through the little boy's head.

How I do it does not need to be how you do it

The couch cuddle, the car chat, the table talk, the bedtime stories, and the just-in-time are the most typical settings I have used to tell case stories to Jupiter. There are others, of course, that you can create. It is *your* job as a parent or a caregiver to figure out which works the best in your situation. The key is to jump in and try, and keep it simple!

One of my friends, Olivia, is a nanny, and the four-year-old girl she cares for is Aida. When Olivia arrives at work in the morning, Aida wants her to tell her stories about her lovey, the Penguin, while she eats breakfast. Olivia tells case stories about the Penguin making the same wise decisions and doing the same good behaviors that Aida did the day before. Aida cannot get enough of the indirect pats on the back. They encourage her. It has become a pleasant way for them to start the day. It is not even a secret any more that the stories are about Aida. Aida enjoys the reinforcement of her good behavior choices, who wouldn't?

8. When It Did Not Work

When the case method didn't work, I learned the most

If it was not for the trials and errors in my own parenting with the case method approach and for the lessons I learned from friends trying it, this book would not be in your hands.

When the case method did not work I learned the most. The detours and the weaknesses in applying it revealed and confirmed the underlying principles and the wisdom behind the approach. The more I spoke with my friends and listened to how they were employing the case tactics, the more I understood what worked and what did not.

One of the outcomes of the trials and errors was that I was able to systematically assemble the second part of this book, the methodology, or the how-to-do-it. It is a guide to building cases that work, using proper tactics. But when all is said and done, it is not going to run its course perfectly every time. But overall, it works!

On occasion, the failures had nothing to do with how I or someone else was implementing the case method. The problems were outside the methodology. Whenever the case method was not working, the first question I asked was whether I was using the proper methodology. If I decided I was, something else was causing the problem.

Usually the problem was the transfer. The transfer problem occurred when Jupiter knew the wise decision for the case protagonist, but he did not own it and do it himself. Sometimes, no matter how many case stories I told him he did not see the wise course. Unfortunately, I have no single formula to deal with this issue in every case. As you can imagine, every case is different, and maybe you are able to address it in your own creative way.

What I learned was that there were times when prior circumstances worked against Jupiter making the preferred decision. I could see times when it was hard for him to make a wise decision due to his experiences earlier in the day. He had not been supported in making the wise decision. In such as case, in retrospect I should have removed the obstacles making it hard for Jupiter to make wise decisions.

Picky eating is not always a choice of the moment

Let me share an example where my parental choices meddled with Jupiter's ability to choose wisely. Let's say I have fed Jupiter snacks on demand all day, and then he refuses to eat his dinner. I have not supported him in making the wise decision to eat a healthy dinner. Jupiter is not hungry. His prior experience—that I could have controlled—is working against what would normally be a wise decision. Furthermore, he may be thinking that it is not even a wise decision to eat dinner when he has been eating all day—and he might be right!

Let me illustrate further with two examples from my own experience. In each instance I applied the case method to help Jupiter make a wise decision. But it did not accomplish anything to help Jupiter own up and make better decisions. It flopped, and I was disheartened. I thought about it more and realized that the case method was not the problem, I was. Once I started making wise decisions to create a supportive environment, Jupiter was able to do his part.

At age two, Jupiter was becoming a picky eater. I did not like it, but I was torn. On one hand I believed it was beneficial for him to eat a diet with a variety of healthy foods. Furthermore, I had read studies about how our eating habits as children translate into adulthood. Children who mostly eat only what they want, say cereals, cheese sticks, pasta, and pizza, and who are not encouraged to expand their taste familiarities, tend to wind up with limited and unhealthy eating habits as adults. On the other hand I knew many children were picky eaters, some more than others, so I partly accepted it as the way children behaved at that age.

After all, many restaurants do it. They offer separate children's menus with pasta and "mac and cheese." Since

Jupiter did not like dill on top of grilled salmon, I would just leave his portion of the salmon without the dill. I was accommodating and making exceptions for him. It backfired. I was having to adapt to Jupiter's preferences more and more. He was in charge and I was following his orders!

I knew I did not like where we were heading, so I started telling Jupiter wise and unwise decisions about how and what to eat at the dinner table. Nothing changed.

One afternoon a friend suggested, "Maybe he is not hungry." I heard her; the issue could be as simple as that. I explored the idea. When did my son eat? How many times a day? What kind of snacks did he have? How often? Did he get enough exercise that day? At the same time I tried to put myself in Jupiter's shoes. Was I picky? When was I picky? Why would I be picky? I dug deeper. The surest way to kill my appetite for dinner was snacking, not only right before dinner but during the day. The first offender to prevent my son from making a wise decision at dinner was the snacks. We eliminated everything but a small snack, a yogurt or a fruit in the late afternoon.

The second offender was the choices I gave Jupiter at dinner. I had to stop making exceptions for him. By giving him what he preferred when he did not like what was offered for dinner, wasn't I training him to become a picky eater? I decided that at three years old most of the dishes Mark and I ate would be good for Jupiter. I put the dill back on the entire piece of the salmon. It was part of the dish I had formulated. I stopped accommodating for Jupiter. If he preferred a sorbet cup for dessert instead of the fruit salad I had already prepared, I did not give it to him. We were having fruit salad that evening. We would have sorbet cups another evening. If Jupiter chose not to eat very much, I allowed it. What I did not allow was for him to eat a snack before going to bed that night.

I would not call my son a picky eater today. He can pick and choose when he has a choice, such as in a restaurant, but when we have a set dinner prepared at home, he knows to try most of the items. The case method did not work because I had been setting up my son for the unwise decisions. Refusing to eat much or only picking what he liked was the natural choice for him because he was not that hungry. He had been snacking all day. He was a casualty of the course of events throughout the day that pulled him to the unwise decision at the moment of choice at dinner. Asking myself what role I played in the dilemma helped to get to the root cause.

Temper tantrums may not always be a matter of choice

When Jupiter was in kindergarten, he had reading homework every day. He was learning sight words and how to sound out the letters. The problem was that whenever he did not recognize a word in his reading homework, he got frustrated and started grunting, making faces, and stomping his feet. He wanted me to help him to sound out the words to figure them out. He got further upset if I pushed him to do it on his own. It was a daily traffic jam as those mystery words showed up in every book Jupiter tried to read. It did not help to explain to him that not every word was a sight word.

I tried the case method because it seemed Jupiter was making an unwise decision by throwing a fit when he did not recognize a word by sight. He also made an unwise decision, or so I thought, when he kept asking for my help every time he was not able to decode a word he saw.

I told him a few cases about a little boy who was learning to read. The cases entailed a boy who chose the wise approach to reading by sounding out words and a boy who threw a fit or made grunts when he did not know how to crack a word. Jupiter knew the wise way for the case protagonist and was clearly thrilled to identify it, but he was not making the transfer. I resolved something else was going on and started exploring what it might be.

I talked to the teachers. They explained the strategies they used at school to help children become independent at decoding unfamiliar words. The strategies included Chunky Skunk, Stretchy Snake, and Skippy Frog. Jupiter was familiar with them. We tried. Yet the issue remained. Jupiter seemed to lack confidence to figure it out on his own.

It was all the more puzzling because Jupiter did not have this issue with math and numbers. With math problems he happily pushed himself to ever more challenging problems. Also, when he was building something, whether with Playmobil, blocks, or Legos, he hardly ever showed exasperation the way he did with the reading exercises. The distinction was that Jupiter was somewhat a natural with construction of three-dimensional structures and math. He liked those activities, they came relatively easy for him. He had confidence he could follow through with those tasks. Not so with adding up letters into words. Why did he lack confidence in one but not the other? I paused to consider what *I* could be doing to contribute to the situation.

Late one night I went through my notes from a class I took and did some digging on the internet. I found out the dependent learner problem was often planted by parents during the third and the fourth years of the child's life. The suggestion of one parenting approach was that the seeds of a dependent learner are planted during the times when the parents show the child—with their behavior—that they do not think the child has what it takes to do what he is supposed to do, especially when it is hard for the child. The example they gave was the morning routines to get ready for daycare or preschool. When well-meaning parents keep reminding the child what he has to do and should be doing, the child is getting a message that he depends on the parents to get ready. The child determines he cannot do it on his own. This subtle message is attitude-changing for the child.

Humility and self-examination help us learn, even our blind spots

Had I done that? I thought through our mornings getting ready for school. Did I trust Jupiter to get ready and take care of what he needed to do on his own? Or did I keep nagging him all the way until we were out the door? I had to admit I did more of the latter. I felt defensive. My justification was that I wanted him to be on time and have his hair straight and face clean. I wanted to show him that in our family we show up on time. Perhaps it had a cost attached to it. Maybe I was creating a dependent learner. I needed to change what I was doing.

Jupiter and I had a discussion. I asked him whether he thought he was a baby or a big boy. I asked him how I helped him when he was a baby, and if I should keep doing that when he became a big boy. We talked about who was in charge of various things in his life. The conclusion was that Jupiter was a big boy and that I had been treating him like a baby when getting out of the house in the morning. We agreed I should not do that anymore. We talked about what he needed to do before going to school in the morning. Jupiter identified every responsibility. He decided he would make a list of all the things he had to do and tape it on his mirror in the bathroom.

I asked him what I could do to help him to know the time to do each task to get him ready to leave on time. We decided to use my phone as the reminder for him to start getting ready after having breakfast. He wanted a certain piece of music to start when it was time to finish breakfast and start brushing his teeth, another when it was time to transition to getting dressed, and still another when it was close to departure time. I set up the phone. Jupiter knew how to make this fun!

It took a few weeks to work itself out. I let Jupiter take care of himself in the mornings without my constant reminders. He took great pride in showing up at the door, ready to go, sometimes even before it was time to go!

With the reading homework, we started including some easier books to help him read some of them straight through without getting stuck. I also taught myself a few of the rules they had about decoding the words, something I had never learned since I grew up and learned to read in Finnish before even taking English. Mixing up the easier books with the challenging books also helped. We no longer had the dependent reader problem.

The case method had failed to solve the problem because Jupiter was not supported in making the wise decision when faced with deciphering unknown words. It helped when I could help him remember the tools and then pull away, letting him do it on his own, praising him for his efforts.

Previously, with my behavior in the mornings as we were getting ready for school, I had been hinting to him that he does not have what it takes to do it on his own, he needs me. I had been communicating that to him via the way I reminded and nagged him in the mornings. Both the reading situation and the morning process were challenging for him, unlike building a tower or adding up numbers. I was telling him, with my behavior, that he needed my help in the challenging tasks of his life. Once I stopped my behaviors that were hurting Jupiter's confidence in himself, he started trusting he has what it takes to complete even the challenging tasks. He saw how he was able to manage himself even when tackling challenging words. I concluded I was the one who had been the one making unwise decisions. Problems are often easier to solve when we look to uncover our role in creating the problem, rather than pointing a finger.

If the case method does not seem to work, the problem may be in the way we employ the method or the problem may lie elsewhere. Once the methodology checks out, we have to look in another place for contributing factors. My next step has been to ask what role I may have played in creating the dilemma. I may be the problem, or at least some share of it. The best part about being the problem is that I can do something about it. I can do something about me and my choices. It also helps to ask questions what else might be taking place that connects to the dilemma. Wisdom and learning often come the best from mistakes and when things go wrong. So it is with the case method.

9. Training Champions

Training athletic and wisdom champions share some tricks

How do you learn? Does imagining yourself doing something help you do it better in life? How is it that when your child puts himself into another child's shoes in a case story, he is then prepped to take that same course of action in real life? How does it work?

I was pondering these ideas as I witnessed the effectiveness of the case method. I drew a parallel to athletics. In certain aspects, the case method for teaching wise decision making to children seems to work in a similar way to learning sports. Both the case method and learning a sport include repeated drills and visualization to achieve mastery.

Mastering moves in sports requires repeated drills

First, repeated drills help master a sport. I ran track as a teenager in Finland and then completed my running career as a full scholarship athlete at Georgia Institute of Technology in Atlanta, Georgia. As a middle distance runner my main event was the mile and the 1,500 meters. I did a variety of running drills to perfect my running form. Each drill was focused on improving a specific part of my stride. I repeated each of these drills over a distance, say fifty yards, two to three times during each training session. The purpose of the drills was to help nail the correct pathways and movements at each stage of my running stride. Pulled together the drills helped me to run efficiently and not waste energy.

During the race when it mattered, these correct pathways had been established in my brain and the muscles controlling the movements. Less effort and concentration was required to run optimally; it had become more or less automatic. Muscles have memories—golfers understand this perhaps better than anyone else—and perfecting movements with repeated drills makes sense in athletics. What I had done with the drills was to divide the more complex running stride into its simpler components and then practice doing each of the components correctly. Mastering the components improved the more complicated whole.

It's largely the same with learning to make wise decisions as a child. Choosing to make wise decisions is like a muscle that can be trained to work a certain way. And, we learn larger wholes by learning them piecemeal. Wise and unwise decision cases are like running drills, and the self-reliant, gritty child is like the efficient runner. Just as mastering rudimentary drills that mimic portions of the running stride helped me run more efficiently, mastering simple wise versus unwise decisions focusing on one area at a time builds the child's insight into what is wise and unwise, his will to do what is wise, and his self-reliance in real life. As we add several types of wise and unwise dilemmas together, we build a self-reliant, independent child.

Imagery training can become a self-fulfilling prophesy in sports

Second, Olympians and champion athletes have long used visualization to master their sport. They visualize themselves in the race situation, they imagine feelings of confidence, fear, and pain as they come and go before and through the race, and they picture the interaction with their competitors. This is called imagery training. The more the athlete can imagine the details, the better he performs in the real event. The athlete can walk into the real event as if he has gone through it before. The debilitating nervousness is removed, replaced with adrenaline-filled excitement, which in turn helps push superior performance.

In my case it went like this: I would imagine myself preparing for the mile race. I am warming up and see my top competitors. I watch them and feel good about being ready. I do my stretching and consciously block out the world.

Every fiber in my body is ready, geared for the four plus minutes it takes to run the race. I feel the nervousness and choose to fill myself with relaxed and focused confidence. I walk to the starting line, lean forward, wait, then hear the gun go off. I visualize every lap, the splits, who is in the race, and finally, the last lap. I imagine how it feels in my legs, but choose to keep my mind on the race. One goal. I picture myself passing on the last curve. I am tired, but I can fly. I imagine that feeling taking over.

Going through the race by visualizing it would prepare me. While picturing the ideal way to run and experience the race setting, I prepped the pathway in a desired direction. The case method works the same way. As your child imagines himself in the shoes of the decision-maker, then feels and experiences the case dilemma, your child opens up the pathways in real life choice-making.

There is power in the imagination. Champion athletes and Olympians use it to win, you can certainly help your child use it to gain wisdom, self-reliance, and grit. In fact, children's imaginations are so alert that appealing to them is just plain easy! For them, the "I think, therefore I am" becomes "I imagine, therefore I can."

"I imagine, therefore I can" becomes true for your child

The demonstration of how this works with the case method is the miracle. From visualization of the case stories and the decision dilemmas, your child moves to making wise choices in his own life. The miracle takes place when your child consciously stands up to make a wise decision instead of going with the flow. The miracle takes place when your child has developed enough self-concept to realize the moment of choice, the time to pause and make a call to do something rather than stand in the sidelines. Grit is the strength of character it takes to do that.

Jupiter told me about an incident at school. He did not share it during the ride home from school when I usually ask him about his day. He voiced it spontaneously later in the evening.

He just came to me and said, "Mommy, can I tell you something?"

"Of course," I responded.

Jupiter continued, "I made a wise decision today. It was a little hard. We were playing a game with balls. There were three balls in the game. Everybody was playing. Then I saw Lucy walk away. Her face was red and she did not look happy. She looked like she was going to cry. I knew she was sad about something. Maybe somebody had been mean to her. I saw an extra ball. I had an idea. But I almost didn't do it. My idea was to take one of the balls to her. I stopped. Then I decided to do it. I got the extra ball and took it to Lucy. I asked her if she was all right. I made a wise decision."

I was so encouraged to hear how Jupiter had chosen on his own to do what he had decided was the wise decision. I embraced it. I commended him, "You were able to make a wise decision even when it was hard. You had to leave the play to go help Lucy!"

For Jupiter this was a small victory, but a part of building his character. He was becoming a wisdom warrior.

Your job is to support your wisdom warrior, just like a coach's job is to encourage his champion-in-training

I realize that there are other ways to assess what happened. The cynics may say that I do not know the details. That is true. What if it was Jupiter who had hurt Lucy? What if he did not tell me that he took the ball from Lucy and only gave it back to her? What if it was not even Jupiter but someone else who did the good deed and he just claimed it was him? Maybe the teacher told Jupiter to get Lucy another ball. The cynics also may say any child could do that even without being exposed to the case method.

Nevertheless, you cannot afford to express doubt to your child about his account of a wise decision. Often, you will see him make a wise decision and there will be no doubt. When he spontaneously shares a story of one you don't see, that is not the time to become skeptical.

When you are training a wisdom champion, planting seeds of doubt and distrust is wrong, plain unsuitable. Certainly, champions-in-training must go through hardships and make mistakes. Doubt will occasionally fill them like a murky liquid. However, as a parent or a caregiver, you are the trainer who is to encourage your child and show him the way. You are the master for the little warrior of wisdom. A master believes in his warrior, his capacity and his capabilities. As you train your child for the path of making wise decisions, you are to show him in what you say, do, and think that you believe he has what it takes. There may be other doubters and skeptics, but you should never be on their side.

My coach never fed me with his doubts about my talents or capacity to handle a workout. He encouraged me and said, "You can do it." There were times when I had doubts about myself, "Do I have what it takes to compete at the national level?" I am so glad I had a coach who refused to join in or feed that conversation inside my head. I reached a lot of my goals as a runner, but not all of them. A few times I made some serious strategic mistakes during a race, costing me participation in the nationals. This is where having an insightful coach who believed in me was crucial. Those mess-ups were simply rocks on the path. I stumbled, maybe fell down, but I was never incapacitated.

Your role as a parent or a caregiver in teaching wisdom via the case method is similar to that of a coach training a champion athlete. However, while not every child is made to become a champion athlete, any child can become a wisdom warrior, or a wisdom champion. Your child does not need to have any talent or score high on some intelligence test. You already know high intelligence does not correlate with wise decision-making in life. The key is that your child simply learns to make wise decisions with what he has and where he is. You act like a championship coach, feeding your child with seeds of trust, constantly watering him with encouragement, and challenging him so those seeds sprout and grow tall and strong in character. This is something every parent can do. You can.

I choose every day to be a wisdom champion-builder by having faith in Jupiter and showing it. I make mistakes. I spew a hasty word that tears down my child. I ask for forgiveness. Jupiter knows I am not perfect on this journey. He also knows I try hard. We each allow for errors: I make allowances for Jupiter, sometimes he will do wrong, and he makes allowances for my errors, sometimes I will do wrong.

Wisdom is more valuable than a championship in some athletic competition. It carries your child through his entire life, and by pursuing wisdom he will experience true happiness.

10. Forming Habits

Repeated thoughts have consequences

Who we are is a combination of what we think and what we do. "Sow a thought, reap an act; sow an act, reap a habit; sow a habit, reap a character; sow a character, reap a destiny," the saying goes. It is formidable to think how our thoughts, when multiplied, turn into destinies. Habits, what we tend to think and do every day, make us into who we are. They form over time. They are etched in the neural pathways in our brains. This allows us to carry them out without consciously thinking of a choice. We simply execute the imprinted directions in our brains.

Then, we'd better have the right thought habits etched in the brains of our children! Making a difference is easier in the small thoughts than in the more significant ponderings. Pushing for change in the little thought habits help direct your child's thinking in the more complex questions later.

For example, if your child learns to focus on his own responses instead of what other children do to him, it might change his entire destiny from that of always being a victim of this and that versus a man who knows what he can and cannot control in his life. When Jupiter was just learning to talk, I used to give him a standard response when he came to me telling what someone had done to him at the playground. I would immediately prompt Jupiter to turn it around in his head by saying, "What did *you* do?" Instead of dwelling on the details of being a victim, it effected Jupiter to change the focus to *his* response. What was important was how he responded, not what someone else did.

A few repeated pushes from me to change his attention was pretty simple to do, and what a difference it has made to Jupiter and to me! Rarely do I have to listen to Jupiter complaining about anyone at school. Instead we can focus on how to handle various situations. He knows he is mostly in charge of what he does and how he responds. Jupiter also knows he will never get a finger-pointing friend in me, so he does not bother.

Starting out small and simple is the most effective way to build habits

Studies show that to form a habit most effectively it is wise to start out with small steps and keep it simple. Adopting more complex behaviors takes longer, and there is a higher chance of getting derailed. For example, it is much easier to focus on having a glass of water with every meal than to do all of the following: drink more water, eliminate soda drinks and alcohol, start an exercise routine every morning, and take up a healthier diet. Better to start with a small step before taking a leap.

The principle behind my case method is the same. To make the cases most effective, it is important to keep them simple, short, and focused. Keep the cases so simple you only focus on one issue in each case. Focus on getting that one dilemma solved. There is no need to introduce a mob of variables to complicate things. It may be too much to bear.

For example, if I am trying to show Jupiter that lying is unwise, then it is more effective to keep my cases focused on lying only and not muddy that choice by venturing into other problems surrounding the lying situation. If my goal is to instill "never tell a lie" in Jupiter, then when I tell him a case story, it should be simply about a little boy who tells a lie. Jupiter's job is only to recognize the lie as an unwise or a wrong choice on behalf of the boy in the case.

I think it is best to pick one rule or one topic and start ridiculously small. You can introduce additional issues later, such as the consequences of lying, but preferably not at the beginning. Once your child answers correctly that it is a wise decision to "never tell a lie" in a simple case over and over again, a habit of choosing to make the wise choice of telling the truth is created. At first, it is not the change in your child's behavior that is important, but that he gets into the habit of picking the right, or the wise, choice in the simple case of lying or not lying. The focus is to get a small step established, to make progress, and avoid getting overwhelmed at any cost.

Telling the truth becomes a habitual wise choice. Then, if your child starts asking questions about the lying and surrounding issues after the case story that is a win in itself. Engage, by all means. The key here is to keep the case itself simple and drive home the wise choice time and time again. Repetition creates the habit, like muscle memory for an athlete. The case method miracle here is that your child starts to "never tell a lie" in his own life.

Believing in the significance of the every-day choices your child has to make
"Little boys have little problems, while big boys have big problems," a friend told me. I agree it seems like that to us. The little boy problems seem inconsequential.

However, I'd suggest that those trivial-sounding problems do not sound so trivial to your little child. Think about that example of "never tell a lie." As a parent you might be tempted to overlook the little lies as insignificant. What is the big deal if your child lied about having washed his hands before dinner? Or if he took a dollar bill from the table to buy candy, thinking a dollar is not so much money for you, and denies doing it? I say these are big deals. Maybe not to you and me, but in his world your child has gone against his most significant authority, his parents, and chosen to tell a lie to avoid facing the consequences. How would this look like in a professional work setting? Maybe the little boy's problems are not so little, after all.

When your child gets into the habit of telling the truth about small things, he will likely tell the truth about more significant events later—precisely because a habit is formed. Your child is actually "good" at telling the truth and "bad" at telling lies, because he has not done it. He lacks skill at lying! So he is much less likely to do it. His habit takes him in the other direction.

Another way of saying this is that those who can be trusted with little can also be trusted with much. When your child finds joy and learns to make wise decisions for someone else in the case, then assumes those behaviors himself, he will likely continue on that path as his life gets more and more complicated. This has powerful implications for your child's future.

You do not need big wins for good habits to spill over

Good habits have a ripple effect that works to your advantage, the small good habits you have incorporated into your life carries over to other aspects of your life.

For example, once you start exercising regularly you start eating better without even thinking about it, become more productive at work, and perhaps even start acting more kindly toward your family. This spillover effect seems to work the same way when your child learns to make thoughtful choices.

Shortly after I had introduced the wise and unwise decision case stories to Jupiter when he was barely three years old, I spotted him doing the right thing on his own in areas we had not even touched with the cases. I saw Jupiter allowing a friend to play with his toy first, and when I praised him for it, Jupiter simply said, "Mommy, I made a wise decision." He knew how to make a wise decision about being kind. Now he was applying that principle to making a wise decision about sharing on his own without even trying. It just spilled over since he knew sharing toys was the kind thing to do. The wise-decision making in one area of life spreads across to other areas.

I believe there is power in the art of small and simple. You want a bigger result? The ripple effect of small good habits will get you there. Cases are most effective and the outcome is the most powerful for the amount of effort put in when you narrow your focus and keep it straightforward.

Forming good decision-making habits empowers your child to become his own person, ever present and mindful about the choices he makes

Case stories, the way I have suggested their use in this book, help you to train your child to lead a fulfilling life early by showing him how to think for himself and make his own wise decisions. Your child makes a habit of stopping to think and consider. Your child makes a habit of growing the mental discipline needed to focus and make thoughtful choices. He makes a habit of becoming mindful at decision points. He makes a habit to push for what he believes is right, wise, brave, or another aspiration. He develops the elusive grit and ability to stand up for what he believes.

It is wise to start engaging your child with the cases when he is young. It is a lot easier to start good habits than change bad ones. Keep the cases focused, simple, and short; the art of the small. However, if you start working on good habits or wise decisions later, it just changes the nature of the cases and the engagement. The key idea is the same. You help your child own his choices and guide his pursuit of wisdom. You engage your child to think for himself. He owns his choices that become his destiny. It is his life.

11. Ever-Changing Brain

Brain science supports the case method miracle
As you engage with the case method you will witness changes in behavior. What you cannot see are the changes inside the brain. But they are there!

How we learn at the brain cellular level sheds some further light on the case method miracle and how it brings about change. Neuroplasticity is a term that refers to our brain's ability to change. Brains cells are also called neurons. Plasticity denotes a characteristic of being easily changed. The brain changes by growing new brain cells, restructuring existing brain cells, or by changing connections between the brain cells. Amazingly, it does this quite spontaneously to become more efficient and effective at getting things done. Neuroplasticity studies show how we learn and unlearn at the cellular level.

Neuroplasticity research yields four fascinating realities that help to explain what takes place inside the brain to make the case method so universally successful. First, our brains change throughout our lives, not just when we are growing up. Second, different types of changes dominate at different periods in our lives and are less dominant during other periods. Third, the neural connections are built or changed from both thinking and doing. Fourth, the environment plays a major role.

Our brains transform throughout our lives; the case method can impact change at any age
The first reality is that we learn new things and unlearn old things throughout our lives. As the brain ages the neural connections we use grow stronger, while the ones we rarely use get weaker or die.

This gives us hope because we can always start anew. If we have made a mess in an area in our lives, we can always try again and learn to apply wisdom the second time around.

If we have learned a bad habit, we can unlearn it. If we can wire it in, we can wire it out. If we can become something we want, we can also de-become something we do not want.

The case method works with any age group because the brain can change itself at any age. You can use the case method to create wise thinking in early childhood, and you can use it with your older children to strengthen wise decision-making and weaken the neural pathways that lead to risky behaviors.

Since Socrates first started using the case method with his adult students, it has risen to prominence in teaching young law and business students around the world. Having experienced how it works at Harvard Business School, seen how they use it at law schools, and applied it with children, I have no doubt it will work with any other age group as well. For example, for teenage dilemmas, you just have to alter the discussion format and the case stories so they are relevant. The case method is applicable at any age when the brain is still learning.

The brain grows the fastest in childhood, but synaptic pruning makes change possible in adulthood, too

The second reality gets more fascinating. Although our brains change at each age, the changes are different at different periods.

Generally speaking, our brains overproduce capacity in the beginning then keep expanding and perfecting that capacity in later years. The brain produces most of its brain cells, or neurons, before birth. The neurons form most of the connections, or synapses, between themselves in the first couple years of life. Synapses are chemically and electronically induced pathways between the neurons. The combination of the neurons and how they connect creates what we feel and how we think and act to get things done. The brain spends the rest of its life pruning the network of neurons and synapses.

The fetal brain creates about a quarter million neurons every minute, resulting in more than one to two hundred billion at birth. That is a big number. It is how many stars there are in the Milky Way, our galaxy. If I said one number per second and counted to one hundred billion, it would take me about 3,200 years. We can safely say we have a lot of neurons at birth! The question is what we do with them.

In the next phase of our development, between the ages of zero and three, the number of synapses grows faster than at any later time in our life. At birth each neuron has several thousand connections to other neurons. By the time we are two to three years old, there can be 10,000 to 15,000, even up to 200,000 synapses per neuron. In those first couple years the brain grows by establishing the synapses. If the stars in the Milky Way represent the number of neurons, the number of ways the synapses can connect is larger than the number of stars in our universe.

The brain has an amazing capacity to adjust and respond to new requirements. Interestingly, 15,000 synapses per neuron at age two or three is about twice the number found in the average adult brain. The average adult neuron has about 8,000 synaptic connections. What happens after the age two or three is called synaptic pruning. Some of the connections get strengthened, some weakened, and some go away from not being used. However, the brain is full of potential because of all those potential new connections and networks. As it grows by making connections it becomes more effective and efficient for what is needed. This lends unlimited potential to the case method miracle.

Both thinking and doing expand the neural pathways, paving the way for the case method miracle

The third reality about neuroplasticity is that our thinking and actions affect the number and the quality of the neurons and their connections in our brain.

Neurons require a purpose to survive. They need a message to deliver. The neurons that neither receive nor send messages diminish and die. Our experiences, what we think and do, create messages for the neurons to transfer. They determine which connections are strengthened and which are pruned. Those connections that are used the most become the strongest. The connections that are not activated die away. We use it or lose it.

The case method miracle relies on the fact that mere thoughts and imagery can change the neural makeup of our brains. When you describe a case scenario to your child and then ask him what the child in the case should do, your child has to create a pathway or strengthen an existing one in his brain for that choice. Let us assume that the case situation you define for your child is a scenario he has not faced yet, but surely will in the near future. By doing this, you help him create a pathway he will need in the future, when real life presents a similar situation.

Our behaviors start from our *thoughts*. As we think, so we become. So imagining doing something right or refusing to do something wrong is the first step in choosing wisely in real life. The case method miracle takes place when your child starts making mindful, wise decisions in his own life, both in situations that resemble told case stories and in situations that do not. His actions started with his thoughts.

Environmental stimulus impacts brain development
The fourth reality about neuroplasticity is that the environment affects how our brains grow. The environment refers to what is being fed into the growing brain. A brain-invigorating environment creates growth in the brain, whereas a dull environment causes neuron death.

As parents we have a say in the kinds of environments to which our children are exposed and how that particular setting stimulates the brain. For example, there is a big difference to the stimulation of your child's brain when you give him a blank sheet of paper and colored markers or a remote controlled car. Drawing will force your child to use his imagination and create more ideas.

As we grow up we make these choices ourselves. We make decisions about how we spend our time outside of our jobs. Our grown-up brains need stimulation, too. Entertainment does not score well in this category of brain stimulation. We also design the roadmap of our brain, whether in the positive direction by making wise, brave, right, or good choices, or in the negative direction by making unwise, risky, wrong, or bad decisions. The more we take a certain pathway the easier it is to take it the next time. If we repeatedly make risky choices or plant doubt, we veer into negative thought patterns. On the other hand, the less we take a pathway, the less natural it becomes for us to go that way. If I constantly think to myself, "I think I can, I think I can," then it will be my helper thought as I fight to create something new, like writing this book! In the end I can say, "I thought I could, I thought I could."

When we engage our children with case stories we create an environment with intense brain stimulation. When you describe a case and ask questions, your child has to use his imagination in several ways. He has to imagine the situation, the case protagonist, the dilemma; and finally, the moral judgment. You feed your child's brain in the most powerful way, the best you can do for brain development.

Engage in case stories grow your child's brain

The basic principles from neuroplasticity support the case method miracle.

The case method works independent of age because of the tremendous capacity of our brains to change through our lives. The vast number of neurons and their dynamic connections to each other tell us there is no limit to what we can program in and out of our brains.

The case method works in any field where we can imagine ourselves in the scenario solving a problem. Because new neural pathways are generated from just thinking and imagining—no action required—the case method qualifies.

Finally, we have a say in the kind of environment to which we expose our children's brains. And there is probably no more stimulating environment for the brain than engaging in case method learning, or sharing decision-forcing stories.

12. State of Mind to Learn

Our state of mind determines our learning capacity and imagination intensity

In addition to neuroplasticity, there is another area of brain science that might help explain why and how the case method accomplishes its miracle: brainwave research.

Brainwaves are associated with our state of mind. They are not about how we feel, whether happy, sad, or angry, but rather about the level of consciousness, alertness, or responsiveness. Our state of mind also influences our capacity to dream and imagine.

This makes a fascinating connection to the case method miracle because the case method miracle relies on your child's facility to imagine himself in the case scenario. In fact, it seems that the more powerfully your child can envision himself in the case situation, the more potent the learning and the transfer. Interestingly, certain brainwaves are more productive to this kind of visioning than others.

From observable neurons to patterns of electromagnetic waves at various parts of the brain

Brainwaves are not physical entities like brain cells. They are electromagnetic waves not observable with our eyes.

As I've shared, ours brains are made up of billions of brain cells, also called neurons. They use electricity and chemical changes to communicate with each other via connections, called synapses. At any point in time when the billions of neurons send electro-chemical signals to each other, they produce a huge amount of electrical activity in the brain. In fact, one human brain generates enough electricity to power a lightbulb. The synchronized electrical pulses assemble into observable oscillatory patterns, or brainwaves. When scientists observe these forms with an electroencephalography (EEG) machine, they have a wave-like, cyclical shape. The brainwave frequency can be observed with an EEG machine and is measured in cycles per second, or Hertz (Hz).

At any point in time, your brain is filled with many brainwave frequencies in different combinations in distinct locations. It makes your mind states extremely varied with limitless combinations. However, certain frequency ranges dominate at definable levels of consciousness. The slower the frequency the more relaxed your state of mind. Whichever of the frequency ranges is dominant, your brain is said to be in that state of consciousness.

Five main brainwave states dominate at various times during the 24-hour cycle

Scientists have termed at least five of these states. They are called Alpha, Beta, Theta, Gamma, and Delta brainwave states. The state of your mind when you are mostly in Alpha waves is awake but relaxed, in Beta awake and alert, in Theta extremely relaxed and receptive (also sleep when dreaming), in Gamma intense problem-solving, and in Delta deep sleep. These brainwaves are defined by their frequency ranges. Theta waves are the most intriguing from the case method miracle perspective. But let's take a quick look at all types of brainwaves.

The Gamma waves are the fastest frequency of the most commonly identified brainwaves, at 30 to 50 cycles per second. When you are trying to solve difficult problems or come up with a new solution or an idea, much of your brain is in the Gamma frequency. Interestingly most of the Gamma waves disappear when you are put to sleep during surgery (anesthesia induced sleep).

Adults' waking hours are dominated by Beta waves at 14 to 30 cycles per second. You are alert and taking care of our everyday goal-oriented tasks with energy, attention, and concentration. The presence of Beta brainwaves is important in your normal functioning and stability. People with insufficient Beta activity in their brains have shown to suffer from insomnia and depression.

As you lay down to rest or go to sleep, you move from Beta to Alpha wave dominance in your brain. Alpha waves have 8 to 14 cycles per second, a bit slower than Beta waves. You are awake but relaxed and restful. Simply closing your eyes will kick your brain to producing more Alpha waves. Also, when you meditate you tend to be in the Alpha mode.

Your actual sleep wavelengths are called Theta and Delta. Theta waves at 4 to 8 cycles per second are predominant during light sleep when you see dreams and during extreme relaxation while still awake. Some scientists call this state is a twilight state where you experience vibrant visions, inspiration, creativity, and unusual insight. Theta waves are also associated with deep meditation, spiritual experiences, and hypnosis. Many researchers claim the Alpha-Theta border to be the optimal range for programming the mind and creating new ideas because the brain is shown to be very receptive to a lot of information in the Theta mode.

When you are in deep sleep, Delta waves dominate your brain. They are the slowest waves in our list, from 0.1 to 3.5 cycles per second. In this state you are completely unconscious, not even dreaming, and your body is healing itself.

Dominating brainwaves states vary between children and adults

The brainwave states differ significantly between children and adults. Until your baby is about one to two years old his brain operates mostly in the Delta frequency, the slowest in the categories. It is the lowest level of consciousness, deep sleep. Another way to think about this is that your baby is pretty much asleep all the time; he just sometimes has his eyes open, sometimes closed. At this state of mind the sensory and other information from the outside world simply enters into the subconscious mind. There is no judgement or critical thinking involved.

Theta waves start to dominate after your baby reaches two years. Your child's brain is predominantly in the Theta wavelength until he reaches five or six years of age. Theta dominance is the part of his childhood when what is real and what is imaginary gets blurred. Play is at its best. From one or two to five or six is the age range when your child is most programmable and open to enormous amount of learning that stays with him for the rest of his life.

About when your child turns six, the Theta waves start losing out to Beta waves during the normal waking state. During the waking hours adults are mostly in Beta wavelength. For adults Theta is the twilight state when you dream at night, are under hypnosis, or when you experience moments of deep insight or advanced intuition, also called God-moments. You have no conscious filtering of ideas, massive amounts simply flow in.

Since the Theta dominance allows your child to absorb enormous amounts of information and experiences directly into his subconscious mind, it gives the case method mind-boggling potential with him at this age. Your child's brain under six years of age is extremely fertile and adaptive for learning the ropes of life, for you to code in belief systems, cultural norms, moral values, and behavioral customs.

Subconscious super-learning on the Theta waves makes the preschool and elementary years the age of opportunity

The value of this age of opportunity is intensified because whatever your child absorbs in his subconscious during those early years tends to stay with him for a long time. Early childhood experiences can be a source of strength or a heavy burden for the rest of his life.

To understand how that works it helps to look at how your subconscious and conscious minds differ. Your subconscious is the associations and positive and negative identifications that get encoded without much editing from our environment. Your conscious mind is your logical and reasoning mind. They are two separate mind conditions. With reasoning and analytical thinking ability, you control your conscious mind. It is not so with your subconscious. The information that enters your subconscious floods into it without processing or revision. The Theta waves provide the pathway to the subconscious mind. Most importantly, your subconscious mind is what makes up most of who you are. Your conscious mind accounts for the small remaining portion. So, there can be a very substantial return on investment—for years to come—by communicating important values during those early years of parenting when Theta waves are dominant.

An illustration of super-learning is how children learn languages during the preschool years. Many of you have noticed how some preschoolers seem to have a great capacity to master languages. Recall that the children in this age group are operating mainly in the Theta arousal state. It makes it easier for them to learn a new language, because they do not have to study to learn each new word. The Theta arousal state allows huge amounts of new language information to flood into their subconscious without thinking about it much. It seems to be programmed in just from exposure to that language. In fact, it is.

Programming the mind of your child under six is easier than any other age—because Theta brain waves are in charge! That creates a special opportunity for you. In addition, what is programmed into your child's subconscious before he turns six stays with him for the rest of his life. So, there is a much higher return for investment in training your young children versus older children. Less effort, more results. I like that!

So now you know some of the reasons why the case method appears to be such a miracle with young children: the dominant presence of the Theta wavelength during the preschool and elementary years. I don't think that this diminishes the power of the case method with the other age groups, it simply implies you might get more bang for your buck during the preschool and elementary years.

13. Boost Effectiveness with Rewards

Positive reinforcement seals a successful launch

The case method storytelling does not work its miracle without immediate, positive reinforcement for choosing the right answer. I have concluded this from my own experience and from talking with parents and caregivers who have tried the case method with their children. Not giving a prize right away for answering correctly has been one of the top reasons for an unsuccessful launch of the case method miracle. Do not let that happen with your process!

Positive rewards for choosing the right answer help in at least three ways. First, they help make the process fun, giving it momentum. What good does it do if you quit after a few tries? Second, the rewards promote an encouraging environment for learning—a growth mindset—whether your child made a good or bad choice in his own life. You praise your child for *knowing* how to make a wise decision, affirming your love for him via the reward. Third, the rewards are your tool to communicate to your child what he wants the most, your love and approval. At Harvard Business School I wanted to give insightful case answers to gain respect from my professor and my peers. But your child does not want your respect, he wants your love and approval.

Rewards help maintain momentum

Immediate rewards give momentum to continue using the method. You want your child to *want* to do the cases. The challenge for you is to make the process palatable for your child. If he likes the rewards enough, your child will want to hear "wise and unwise decision stories," "stories about a little boy," or whatever it is that you call the case stories. At first, your child may even want the reward more than the story. No matter, the key is to build momentum for the miracle learning to take place.

I have a friend, Leila. Leila takes care of a little four-year-old girl, Jane, during the day. Jane's heroine is Anna from the movie *Frozen*. Little Jane calls Leila "Miss Leila" and adores her. Jane is thrilled when Miss Leila praises her for any small accomplishment or good behavior. Miss Leila began telling Jane stories about Anna. In these stories Anna encounters situations where she makes choices, sometimes wise, sometimes unwise. They are case stories at their best. Little Jane fell in love with the case stories and kept coming to Leila asking her to tell more stories about Anna. What Jane wanted was to hear Miss Leila praising her about how she made wise choices. Little Jane got a thrill from knowing the right answer and being told so by Miss Leila. The momentum comes from the rewards helping make the case story experience positive and fun for the child.

Once the child has bought into the case stories and enjoys them, I have discovered it does not kill the progression to skip the rewards every once in a while, or only use verbal affirmation. For example, after Jupiter had started loving the "wise and unwise decision stories," I started doing them in the car while driving. Initially, while telling the stories on the sofa, I had rewarded him with tickles and kisses every time. I think Jupiter loved the tickling and kisses more than the stories themselves in the beginning. But this wasn't going to work while I was driving! Instead, after Jupiter answered correctly in the car, I praised him for knowing how to make wise decisions. Being praised is a verbal affirmation, a reward too, though maybe not as powerful as tickling and kissing. However, by that time Jupiter was familiar with the "wise and unwise decision stories" and was enjoying the entire process, not just the tickles and kisses.

It pays off to start simple and with powerful rewards that speak love to your child. Once the process is established and your child is enjoying it, you start tinkering and trying greater challenges. Some form of positive reinforcement is crucial in establishing a lasting positive association with case storytelling for your child. The rewards build momentum; they pull your child along for the ride to learn how to make wise choices.

Rewards foster a positive learning atmosphere even when your child has failed

Rewards are also important because they promote an encouraging environment for learning, even in failure. On one hand, it is exciting for your child to know the right answer and feel affirmed with a fun reward. On the other hand, some of the case stories are about situations where the case protagonist has made an unwise decision, exactly the way your child made it. Your child convicts himself as he condemns the case protagonist. He realizes the connection sooner or later. Your child gets it, "Hey that is what I did."

When your child is praised and rewarded for recognizing that the case protagonist made a bad decision, the reward makes a difference. The positive reinforcement for answering *correctly* helps your child deal with the pain and judgment he experiences internally when he realizes he is guilty of the same bad choice. On one hand, it provides your child a way out of the public humiliation and demoralization that can come if you make the failure explicit.

On the other hand, it provides a path for self-examination, self-regulation, and accountability to self. This kind of inner dialogue paves the way to grit, self-reliance, and independence. When your child condemns his own choice from his own inner voice, it seems to motivate him to make the right choice next time more than when external punishment and disapproval has come from you. From the perspective of the brain, making a correct judgment about a bad decision connects a neural pathway in a loving, encouraging atmosphere. New neural pathways are opened from these thoughts, making good behavior more likely in the future.

A friend, Teresa, told me about an embarrassing interchange. She handled it in a way that let Tessa, her daughter, bear the guilt and take responsibility for it. An elderly relative, Ms. Judith, had made a rare visit to the family's home. Before leaving Ms. Judith wanted to take a photo of Teresa, her husband Mike, and Tessa. Tessa had just turned six. She had been playing in their basement when Teresa called her for the photo.

Tessa came up and snapped, "I do not want to be in any photos. Why do I need to be in the photo?"

Teresa and Mike were embarrassed by Tessa's rudeness. Ms. Judith was clearly uncomfortable. They took the photos, but it was not a pleasant situation. Once Ms. Judith had left, Teresa and Mike wanted to speak to Tessa. However, they decided to wait and address it when everyone had calmed down.

That evening after reading a few of Tessa's favorite nighttime stories, Teresa told Tessa a story of her own—a case about a little girl named Laura. Tessa loved *Little House in the Prairie* stories. Laura was an immediate positive connection.

Teresa described, "Once there was a little girl. Her name was Laura. She lived in a farm house in the middle of a prairie. She loved her Ma and Pa. One day they had Pa's sister visit from a nearby town. Her name was Aunt Polly. Aunt Polly and Laura's parents talked with each other all afternoon. Laura got tired of listening to the adult talk. She went off to play with her dolls in the corner of the room. She was in the middle of playing when Aunt Polly was getting ready to leave.

Ma looked at Laura, 'Laura, why don't you come with us and walk Aunt Polly to her carriage?'

Without thinking, Laura snapped, 'Why do you need me there?'

Aunt Polly turned her head and looked at Laura. Her face looked hurt."

Teresa held Tessa close and looked her in the eyes, "What do you think about that? Was Laura kind or rude?" Tessa averted her eyes and did not say a word. After another moment of silence Teresa continued, "How about Aunt Polly? How do you think she felt? We know she loved Laura." Tessa still did not say anything. Teresa took her to her arms, "I love you so much. I love you so much I want to tell you things that you may not even want to hear. I love you. I only want the best for you."

Tessa looked at her mother, "Mommy, I will not do that again." Teresa hugged and held her daughter. Then she read one more story from Tessa's favorite storybook. She did not bring up the incident with Ms. Judith again. She let Tessa process her own behavior.

You can certainly use case stories to show your child his wrong choices, but you should not be the one to point the finger. As a parent it is easy to abuse the case method by using it to draw attention to your child's wrongs. The case method then becomes a way to punish your child. However, no child will want to engage in the case method if the stories are used to point to his wrongs every time. Most of the time your child knows when he has made a wrong decision, and your job is to help him move away from those decisions, not to sink him deeper into the hole by pointing fingers and publically demoralizing him. I have found this hard to do, to keep away from doing the latter.

The most effective way to avoid this is to make sure your rewards are exciting and desirable to your child and by keeping most of your cases as positive behavior examples. It is as straightforward as it sounds. You choose to reward your child with what he likes the best, and you challenge *yourself* to catch your child making *both* wise and unwise choices. Often we are quicker to catch the wrong than the right—because they seem to matter more, to have greater consequences. This gives us as parents and caregivers an opportunity to grow towards a more positive mindset as we work to notice when our children do what they are supposed to do, not just when they misbehave.

Rewards help fill your child's greatest need, your love and approval

The case method used at business and law schools differs from the way I propose to use it with your child. The most effective rewards for correct answers are different, too.

A parent-child or a caregiver-child relationship is rather distinct from a student-professor relationship. I'd suggest that while students at graduate school want respect and dialogue with their teachers, your child mostly desires *to be loved*. A student wants to get good grades and learn, but your child wants love and approval from you. Numerous studies have demonstrated the importance of expressed love between a parent and child. After your child answers the case question correctly, your most effective reward is the kind that communicates love and approval to him.

Rewards are a way to show love to your child. Gary Chapman has discussed how children best receive and express love in *The Five Love Languages of Children*. According to his framework, children tend to have preferred ways to express their love in the same way adults do. The levers vary. Some children express their love clearly in one or two of the five love languages, while others use all five with no clear preference. No matter, it is useful to consider how your child communicates his love and then use that love language to channel love to him. The five love languages to contemplate include verbal encouragement, time together, giving and receiving gifts, doing something for one another, and physical touch. Once you discover your child's main love language or languages, you learn that some rewards are indeed better than others and that each child is different. Applying rewards in your child's love language will help you convey your love for you child most successfully.

You may have seen how some rewards work better than others, and some do not work well at all. Some incentives work with one child, but not the other. A particular reward communicates love to one child, but not so much to another. Because of every child's need for love, the rewards that are most effective are the ones that communicate love. To have the greatest impact in teaching wisdom, you tap into the greatest desire your child has, his desire to be loved. He will want more.

You love your child while you tell the story and you give him a special love shower when he answers correctly. In other words, you design the rewards in terms of your child's natural desire to be loved. Maybe your child collects stickers? Or perhaps he likes collecting check marks for a total of ten to get a lollipop? With Jupiter, I used cuddling and tickling, and later chasing him around the house, but you would be wise to use rewards you think will work the best with your child—rewards that communicate love in the love language of your child. A teacher cannot do this; it requires one-on-one parent attention.

Practical characteristics of the most effective rewards

I discovered that the rewards that worked the best had certain practical characteristics. They should be quick to administer, simple, mutually bonding, and they should communicate love. I think rewards with those traits are most effective as the case method miracle starting incentives.

On the next page is a simple table. I list examples of rewards in the first column. The next four columns list the reward criteria. Consider these examples and the criteria, then add your own perspective for your child by including other reward examples and b placing numerical values in the cells to help evaluate them.

TABLE 1. Reward Examples.

Reward	Quick to administer	Simple	Creates a bonding experience	Speaks love to my child
Praise, "Great job!"				
Affirming the process, "You sure are learning how to make wise decisions!"				
Hugging				
Kissing				
Tickling				
Chasing				
High fiving				
Giving a point towards something the child wants				
A small toy as a gift				
A surprise				
Going to a movie				
Planning to play together				
Having a date together				
Making the child's favorite food				
Inviting friends over				
Going on a bike ride				
Doing mazes together				
Playing a game inside				
Playing a game outside				
Throwing a ball together				
Playing tea party together				

When you evaluate the example rewards in the first column, your rating depends on your child's primary love language. Why would I give Jupiter stickers for every right answer when what he most wants is hugs, kisses, and cuddling? What if it was not the toy your child wanted, but to *play* with you? Since feeling loved is one of the most powerful needs your child has, it pays to explore and identify the rewards that best communicate love to him.

Prefer rewards with more intrinsic than extrinsic value

To further evaluate the incentives and explore how the case method works its miracle most effectively, it helps to classify the rewards into extrinsic and intrinsic.

Extrinsic rewards are material rewards, outside the action or behavior being rewarded. Examples include candy, stickers, money, and other treats or prizes.

Intrinsic rewards are "feel-good," psychic, or internal. They include the feelings of pride or excitement you get when you know you have done a good job.

Both intrinsic and extrinsic rewards work, but how they motivate differs. Many suggest you can get quick results with extrinsic rewards, but if you use intrinsic rewards, you will accomplish a more permanent change.

Your child is intrinsically motivated when he wants to do something because he enjoys it or finds it satisfying in some way. The intrinsic rewards your child receives might be feeling loved, enjoying storytelling, wanting to engage with you, enjoying the feeling of physical closeness that takes place during the case story, or sensing worthiness or independence in knowing the answer.

By comparison, extrinsic motivation refers to behaviors in which your child engages to earn external prizes or avoid punishment. These rewards can be tangible or intangible, but they are outside your child. Getting a sticker when your child answers correctly to the case question is a tangible extrinsic reward. Gaining your approval when answering correctly is an example of an intangible extrinsic reward. Your child can also be acting to avoid punishment, which is an extrinsic motivator.

Let me share a cautionary note about balance. Be careful not to give extrinsic rewards that are oversized for the question or issue. For example, expensive playsets, or promises of them, are inappropriate rewards for answering case stories wisely. Such a reward is a poor fit with the effort required to answer correctly. Once you set such expectations about the reward, the next time you use the case method, you will likely have to set the reward high to match the prior one. Possibly, nothing less will do.

Which is better, extrinsic or intrinsic, tangible or intangible? There is a place for each. I doubt there is a straightforward answer for all situations. Which reward works the best depends on your child, the relationship he has with you, and where he is in the learning process. For adults, simple extrinsic rewards are effective in *starting* a new habit, say exercise, but once you get going with it, it is the intrinsic rewards of exercise that *keep* you with the exercise program. You feel better, sleep better, eat better, and are more productive. Those are intrinsic rewards that motivate you to keep exercising.

Similarly, what I have seen work with case stories is that when a child begins with extrinsic rewards for making wise decisions for someone else, over time—as if a miracle—they transform into internal motivators. The child starts finding satisfaction in making wise choices in his own life. Though the child may start engaging in the case stories from extrinsic rewards, say getting stickers, he moves towards making wise decisions, not just for the case protagonist, but personally for himself in his own life. It is the way of the case method miracle. It turns out that simple extrinsic rewards are the means to the end, the result is that your child becomes intrinsically motivated to make wise decisions in his life.

14. Being Present

Parenting demands and outside pressures distract from being present with your child

Anyone with a child or several of them knows parenting is hard. There are no universal rules or formulas that work every time. In addition, each child is different. What works with one does not work with the other. There are more exceptions and complications than there are consistent rules of thumb. Having tried to build my expertise on parenting from literature and seminars, I have only come to learn how little I know and how many angles there are to approach training a youngster. You may have experienced some of that, too.

You may also want to give your child opportunities to engage in sports or learn other skills such as playing a musical instrument. Finding what to do at a reasonable cost and the right place and time can become a logistical nightmare.

On top of the parenting pressures, you may have to deal with and solve issues from work or finish a work project at home. There are constant demands on our time and our minds, but only 24 hours in a day.

But being a good parent means you have to spend time with your child, especially during the early years. Yet it is hard to be present when you are focused on juggling several tasks at the same time rather than simply being engaged with one another. Fortunately, research has shown that the quantity of time does not seem to matter as much as the quality of that time. This is not to say that quantity does not matter, only that quantity by itself does not mean much if none of it is quality time. You must make the time you spend with your child count.

Sometimes you are physically present but mentally absent with your child. It means that you are physically with him, but mentally stressed out about something else, thinking about other things, or simply engaged in another activity. According to research, if you are present but in fact "absent," and this is the only way you spend time with your child, it would be better to be actually absent. That kind of "there, but not there" behavior appears to be more harmful than supportive. I have done it.

Building any relationship requires active engagement
It is easy to be at hand but not actively involved with your child. For example, you could spend hours watching television with your child or being in the same room with him but engaged with your tablet. The question to ask is how much of the time you spend with your child is simply being present versus keenly engaged. Of course, there is a time and place to wind down and relax with your children; however, if that is the norm of how you associate with your children, you are not providing the benefits that come from showing more active interest.

Quality time is when you are engaged *with* your children in some activity or when you talk *with* them eye-to-eye. Examples include reading with your child, talking with each other about what you have read or seen, discussing your day's experiences, or inquiring from your child about what is going on in his heart. Those quality times of connection are the moments that count in building relationships.

Mark, Jupiter, and I were once on a family trip and developed a ritual to play a card game after dinner every night. We were engaged with each other in the game as equals, sometimes winning and sometimes losing. We were learning to be good sports, to encourage each other, to laugh at ourselves and at each other, and learning to read cues about each other. These were times of quality interaction. The scenarios that developed between us while we played provided materials for case stories at bedtime.

One case story was about a little boy who threw a fit when he lost. Another story was about a little boy who shared encouraging words to his friend when the friend was going down in a game of cards. There was even a story about a little boy who did not like losing a card game and got upset every time he lost but then started learning what it meant to be a good sport. I would not have had those opportunities with Jupiter if instead I had let him play a game on a tablet, on his own.

The face-to-face human interaction is missing when your child plays an electronic game, so is the reading of cues from the faces or expressions of other players. Also, when your child plays a computer game and gets angry at playing poorly there is no other player who gets hurt, notices, or cares—no learning to play well with others occurs.

Finally, having spent the time with Jupiter after dinner, I was there to see what he did and how he responded to situations, giving me material for case stories later. I had to be present and pay attention.

Making organized, outside-of-the-home activities count

One-on-one interaction with the child cannot be delegated to an organized activity outside the home. As parents, we have to be wise judges of how much busyness there is in the family schedule, and if there is adequate time for connecting to ponder life and our inner workings.

If the majority of the time we spend with our children is on the sidelines of the soccer field, then we might ask ourselves whether we are actively involved with our children or the other parents. Too often we mistake parenting with engaging our children with activities outside the home in the name of keeping them busy. Since I cannot, do not have time, or do not know how to spend time with my child, the next best thing to do is sign him up for football, soccer, karate, baseball, ballet, dance, chess, swimming, piano, or gymnastics lessons. We fill our children's every free moment with some kind of organized, adult-led activity. We in turn are busy taking them to and fro, possibly talking to our friends on the phone as we do so. When we are busy with "kid stuff," we somehow think we are doing a good job.

While all those undertakings may be beneficial for the child's skill development in an area, they are poor substitutes for the one-on-one parent interaction with the child. I propose we should regularly evaluate our weekly schedules to make sure we have a balance.

My challenge to us as parents and caregivers is to make wise decisions about how much time to commit to organized outside-the-home activities before they take over our and our children's lives. The more you know what is happening in your child's life, the more ideas you have for case stories.

Case method affords a way to connect with your child about his life

From my experience, using the case method does not add to the parenting load, nor does it present any kind of a new angle to add to what you are already doing. It is simply a way to engage your child in a meaningful way about life. It is a way to have a conversation with your child. It is a way to engage your child to think about decisions he makes every day, *his* decisions. It is a device to be present when it is so easy for us as parents to be there but not be there.

For your child it is a way to push independent thoughtfulness into his choices. It is a way to help him develop self-reliance and excitement about growing up. It is a way to help him develop the all-elusive grit to bear up under difficult circumstances, first under easier ones, then under more complicated dilemmas.

Using the case method with your child helps you to make the time you spend with your child quality time, it helps you to connect. Even if the case is about another child, it opens up avenues of conversation, if not immediately following the case story, then later. The idea is to take the case method and use it your own way in your own circumstances. In no way should using case method stories add to your load, but rather complement what you are doing already and be a tool to use in whichever way you choose to use it. It will work its miracle. It has for thousands of years—since Socrates, the father of the approach!

How much time you spend with your child—and *how* you spend it—is your decision to make. There is nothing your child wants more than your total attention.

II.

Guide:
The 1-2-3 of How to Do It

The beginning of wisdom is the definition of terms.
Socrates

15. Parenting Engineering

Figuring out better ways to be a parent—parenting engineering

I am a Georgia Tech systems engineer by education. I learned about engineering organizations and processes for optimal performance (systems engineering). Other engineering disciplines cover constructing bridges and other physical structures (civil engineering), assembling electrical circuits to make robots and computers (electrical engineering), or formulating chemical compounds to improve foods or medicines (chemical engineering).

But, you do not have to be a trained engineer to have an engineering mind. Most of us have engineering minds in one respect or another. An engineering mind is one that enjoys figuring out better ways to do things. I fit that description and you probably do too.

As a parent you are constantly engineering approaches to parent better. Otherwise, you would not be reading this book! You engineer how to make your home run more efficiently, and how to fit all that needs to be done into your week. You encounter a problem, you do some research and learn about it, you specify what you want and figure out some solutions, you pick the best and try it, you tinker with it, and you have an answer to solve the problem. You are engaged in parenting engineering.

Engineering design process of the case method miracle

Interestingly, I used an engineering design process to refine the case method approach for children.

When I first came up with the idea to apply the case method I had learned about at Harvard Business School to being a parent, I did not have a detailed methodology in mind. I only had a problem I was trying to solve. I wanted a simple and easy way to tackle the everyday issues that came up in raising Jupiter. I assumed that since the case method worked in business education, it would work in training children, too. I believed there were enough parallels between the two to see if it could work. It was the start. It was a possible solution.

Engineering a solution to any problem requires us to work cleverly to bring about a fresh way to address an issue. In my version I made some assumptions, such as drawing close parallels with the business school cases, to guide my design efforts. I tinkered with the approach, tried it out, and kept making it better by getting feedback and incorporating changes. I did some research to see how it made sense from the science perspective. Finally I decided it was time to freeze the design and document it as if a formula or a how-to recipe. This section of the book is the outcome of the documentation.

I could describe the same process from another perspective, perhaps from the way Jupiter saw my storytelling evolve. In the beginning I was reading him story books. Once he had turned two, I started telling him stories from my own imagination. Once I got comfortable as a storyteller, I created two imaginary characters. Their names were Silly Elephant and Sunny Bunny. What was stunning to me at the time was that Jupiter preferred my stories about Silly Elephant and Sunny Bunny to the story book stories. Sometimes I would tell these tales at the playground with other children present. They started begging for my stories, too. The stories were fun adventure accounts.

After a while I wanted to add something to the silliness of my tales, and the idea of incorporating moral lessons emerged. However, Silly Elephant did not seem a fitting character for the moral stories—he was silly by definition—so I began using a generic "little boy." Then as I decided to ask Jupiter about the moral choice the little boy had made in my story, I made the connection to the business school cases. Instead of telling a story about Silly Elephant and Sunny Bunny, I would tell Jupiter about a little boy having to solve every-day dilemmas. They were every-day dilemmas in Jupiter's world, like what to do when mother says it is time to get ready for bed. I observed Jupiter as I was doing this, what worked and what did not. It was trial and error. Since the approach was so simple, I quickly refined my case stories to the point where they started bearing fruit. I noted it was crucial to keep it simple and to reward my son for knowing the correct answer right away.

Communicating results

After I realized how well the case method worked with Jupiter, I started sharing the approach with my friends who had small children. I told them I had taken what I had learned about the case method at Harvard Business School and adapted it to work with my child. Most found the method fascinating and wanted to try it. It was easy to do, simple, and applicable to any situation. Helping their children become independent thinkers appealed to many parents. A few friends and acquaintances also came to me asking me what I was doing with Jupiter, given his independent stance and drive. My three-year-old was making wise choices without my prompting, even when I was not present. Friends noticed this.

Let me share an example of when I first learned how Jupiter was standing up for what he knew was the wise choice, independent of others.

One afternoon I was not able to take him, four years old at the time, to his gymnastics class. I asked a friend to help and take him. Afterwards, she told me what happened.

While the boys were on a short break and were moving to another activity station during the gymnastics class, several of the boys started to sneak over to the area in the gym where they were assembling new equipment. It was a dangerous construction area, taped off limits. The coaches had told the boys to stay away from the taped-off area.

Jupiter stopped and said, "I am not coming. It is not a wise decision. We can get hurt." He had stated it clearly enough for the other boys to have heard it, too. I was impressed. Jupiter had stood up for what was right alone at such a young age.

Tinkering with the approach, freezing the design, and sending it out to the world

Sharing my approach with other parents and caregivers helped gain momentum. I explained how the case method worked at Harvard Business School and how I had modified it to tell case stories to Jupiter.

With a few brave souls willing to try it with their children, I started receiving feedback and questions I was sometimes unprepared to answer. The best part was that I was now improving on my original approach, with other parents and caregivers contributing to the process. With the issues my friends brought up and with the stories they shared about trying the case method, I realized I was synthesizing something universal. The more feedback I received, the more certain commonalities started to emerge.

Furthermore, as I discussed these ideas with my friends and listened to their case story examples and experiences with their children, I started to see a need to document the discoveries. I saw a need to put together some ground rules on how to come up with the cases. Then one friend suggested I should write a formula on how to do it. I needed to take what I had learned and document a structure, formula, and ground rules for the case method. I thought through what the common elements were, the typical pitfalls, and how best to make the cases effective. I came up with what became the three chapters in this part of the book, guiding you on how to put the cases together.

But, trust me, even though there are three chapters, you can easily do the case method. It's not difficult!

16. Structure—What It Looks Like

Five key ingredients make up the structure
Case stories follow a consistent pattern. The main character, the situation, the dilemma, the decision, and the evaluation make up the structure of any case story.

Here, I condense the five key pieces of the structure and illustrate how you can use them to build a case story.

1. **Start with the main <u>character</u>** right away, who it is. Specify the name or use a generic term.
   "Once there was a little boy…"

2. **Describe the <u>situation</u>** from the child's perspective.
   "… He loved his mother. His mother had told him certain rules at the house. One was that the little boy could watch television while Mommy prepared dinner as long as he would come and set the table when Mommy asked for it…"

3. **Define the <u>dilemma</u>** to make a decision, again, from the child's perspective.
   "…The little boy was watching his favorite television program, Jake and the Neverland Pirates. Mommy was preparing dinner. The little boy loved the show. It was funny. It made him laugh. The little boy wanted to see what would happen next. Just then Mommy called out to him, 'Time to come set the table!' But the little boy did not want to stop the program. He wanted to see what was going to happen next in the show…"

4. **Declare the <u>decision</u>** the case protagonist made. Alternatively, leave out what the case protagonist chose to do and ask your child what he thinks would be the wise choice.

"...He did not respond but continued watching. When Mommy called again, the little boy got angry and snapped, 'Let me finish!'"

5. **Ask your child to <u>evaluate</u>** the decision.
   Alternatively, if you left out what the case protagonist chose to do ask your child what he thinks would be the wise choice.
   "...Was that a wise or unwise decision?"
   Or
   "...What should the little boy do?"

17. Formula—How to Build It

In this chapter I share a formula on how to build a case story. You can think of it as a recipe with key ingredients and how to use them to make a great dish, the case method miracle.

I believe the more consistently you practice these principles, the more likely the case method will realize its miracle. However, since the process is both art and science, my formula is suggestive only. Study the formula and the variables and see what makes sense in your family, to your child.

The key variables of the formula include the character, the story, the conclusion, the reward, and the takeaways. In the following pages I recommend how to use each variable for making the case method work its miracle. It is how to include each of the five ingredients into a successful recipe.

1. The main character: Simple and flat.

Make the main character—also called the case protagonist—such that he pulls your child in the story, does not distract from it.

Your child is to quickly and easily identify with the character and then put himself in the case character's shoes. Consider the following:

a. Choose a generic figure, such as "a little boy" or "a little girl" without a name, or Girl A, Girl B, Girl C.

b. Choose a hero your child admires or with whom he identifies. Even better, let your child choose the character, a character there is no need to describe, such as Luke, Finn, or Rey from Star Wars, Jake from The Neverland Pirates, Anna from Frozen.

c. Avoid choosing a friend or someone your child knows. The idea is for your child to identify with the main character, but not open doors to finger pointing. Your child won't identify with someone he knows personally, he will think the story is simply about that child.

2. The _story_: A single incident that mimics your child's immediate experience.

Focus the case on one idea, one choice, from the _child's_ perspective.

The idea is to create clarity, simplicity, focus, and quick wins. Keep in mind the following points as you build your story:

a. Guide your child to focus on making wise decisions in well-defined scenarios, not in setups filled with confusion. These are not Harvard Business School cases where every option has to be considered and debated, and where the student has to pull out the important from the unimportant. Let that come later.

b. Life situations involve more noise and distractions than the case stories. However, if your child has learned to choose wisdom for the main character in a simple case story, it is easier for him to eliminate the noise in real life and focus on the choice at hand.

c. Make your case instruct on a single point. Your case could be about sharing a toy with a friend or about choosing to tell the truth, but not both of those issues in one case. If you want to address both issues, tell two separate cases, one about sharing a toy and the other about telling the truth.

Tell your story from the child's perspective, not yours. This is harder to do than you think, ponder the following:

a. The more you can stick with telling the facts of the situation, the better.

b. Avoid expressing your feelings or view about the situation.

c. Stay away from our "holier than Thou" mountain top from where you lecture your child via the case story. It is easy to fall prey to it. It is a trap.

d. Evaluate how the next two descriptions, i and ii, are different. The first case is from the mother's perspective, the second from the child's perspective.

    i. The little girl was playing with her rocket ship. Mommy had just cleaned up the play area and finished the laundry while the little girl was at school. Mommy was tired. They had already had a talk about putting toys back in the right places the week before, so Mommy expected the little girl to obey that agreement. When it was time to leave for the friend's birthday party, the little girl was ready to go. She jumped up and rushed to get her shoes and jacket. She forgot all about putting the doll back in the drawer.

    ii. Mommy was reading the paper. The little girl was playing. The little girl was so excited about her new doll. She loved playing with it. She was also excited about going to her best friend's birthday party at her favorite indoor playground. She could hardly wait. The little girl was in the middle of her play when Mommy said it was time to get ready to go to the birthday party. Finally, time to go! The little girl got so excited to get dressed up she dropped the doll on the floor and rushed to get her jacket and her shoes.

The key to telling your story from the child's perspective is to describe what the child is experiencing without pointing out what others are thinking. The child would not know that. Tell what all the characters *do*, and when it comes to what they *think*, limit your sharing to the thoughts of the child who faces the dilemma. If you want to introduce empathy, you can, but do it from the child's perspective.

You can make up the case scenario from the past or the future. You can tell a story from what recently took place in your child's life or from encounters you anticipate in the near future. Consider the following:

a. A case could be a situation your child recently experienced and made a wise decision. You describe the situation as a case story as if it happened to another child and show how he made a wise choice, thus affirming your child.

b. A case could be a situation your child already experienced and made an unwise decision. You describe the situation as a case story as if it happened to another child and show how he made an unwise choice, ushering your child to realize what he did.

c. A case could be a description of situation before your child has experienced it, something you expect him to go through in the near future. The idea is to prepare your child to act wisely.

d. A case could also be a description of a situation you have heard another child having gone through, and you want to pre-expose your child to help him handle it wisely.

The younger the child, the shorter the case. The following includes some principles about the length:

a. A rule of thumb for the length:
   - Rarely over a minute for 2-5 year olds, mostly under ½ minute.
   - Mostly around a minute for 6 years and up, sometimes over a minute.
   - Effective cases can be less than ½ minute long; a quick, to the point, simple choice.

b. Rather err on keeping the stories too simple than embellishing to make them sound better.

c. More mature children can handle longer stories without getting distracted beyond the central idea.

d. A serial case is an exception to the length.
   - In a serial case you ask questions along the way as the main character makes choices. You progress the story after the question, answer, and reward.

- Still, keep it simple and focused the character having made one choice per question.
- Loading up and asking all the questions in the end of a long case story risks unnecessarily complicating the matter.
- I avoid using serial cases, but have witnessed them work.

3. The _conclusion_: A question and call for action.

Your case is not a case unless there is a call for a decision—what action the main character should take—in the end.

I have categorized the case endings into three different conclusions, or calls for action. The call for action can be to judge a decision made, to choose from several options, or to formulate a plan of action. The following summarizes how to do the three case endings:

a. To judge a decision made: "Did the little boy make a wise or unwise decision?"

- This question is the easiest to answer, an excellent way to start with your child.
- A few alternatives to using wise or unwise include the following:
  - Right or wrong
  - Good or bad
  - Brave or cowardly
  - Thoughtful or inconsiderate
  - Mindful or forgetful
  - Kind or rude

b. To choose from several options: "Which of them made the wise decision?"

- Cases where you tell the same situation 2-3 times each time with a different character choosing a different decision.
- Your child does not have to formulate a solution, only to pick the right one.

- For example, here is a case about how to respond to a bully at the playground:
  "Once there was a bully at the playground. She was mean and yelled at the other children. The bully yelled at Girl A. Girl A ran to her Mommy, crying. So that was Girl A. The bully yelled at Girl B. Girl B decided to yell back and started hitting the bully. Girl B was angry and wanted to hurt the bully. Finally, there was a third girl, Girl C. The bully yelled at Girl C, but Girl C responded by saying, 'Well, that is not a nice thing to say. I will not play with you.' Then Girl C turned around walked away from the bully. She did not look back. She quickly figured a fun thing to play with. Which of them made the wisest decision, Girl A, Girl B, or Girl C?"

c. To formulate a plan of action: "What should he do?"

- This is the classic case study. You describe a scenario from the main character's perspective. You end the story with the main character facing a dilemma, what to do. You let your child to formulate the response.
- Keep the cases clear and straightforward. If your child has a hard time formulating a response, your case is too difficult. Simplify.

There is a clear progression from judging a decision already made to formulating one's own course of action. In the beginning you ask your child simple black and white questions. As your child matures, you introduce grey areas and different perspectives to look at dilemmas. It is your delicate experiment to give your child just enough challenge that he can figure it out on his own and have a sense of pride and ownership about having done so. If the cases are too easy too many times, your child will get bored with them. But if the cases are too hard and require too much guidance from you during the problem-solving moment, then you are simply teaching your child, and the miracle of "I did it" is stolen from him.

4. The <u>reward</u>: A quick-to-administer, simple, and mutually-bonding expression of love.

Do not skip the reward, it is crucial for the momentum, the bait and the hook. Please see the chapter on rewards earlier in this book for a comprehensive discussion. The following summarizes how to design them:

   a. Consider what might be your child's love language. In other words, how do you think you communicate love to your child most effectively?

   - Via physical touch: Does he like to be touched and held?

   - Via quality time together: Does he get really excited about playing with you or going somewhere with you?

   - Via gifts: Does he shine the most when he gets stickers or other little gadgets from you?

   - Via words of affirmation: Does he bring you sheets of paper with hearts on them, or write "I love you" everywhere he can?

   - Via acts of service: Does he often ask you to help him fix a toy or clean his room? Does it sometimes feel he is testing your commitment to him by asking for these favors?

   b. Choose the rewards you see working the best with your child. Examples include a hug or a kiss, tickling, time to play together, a love note or a sticky note with hearts on it, praising your child for choosing the wise decision, a sticker for a collection.

   c. Keep the rewards quick and simple to pull your child into the process.

   d. Children's attention spans are short. You must reward right away, otherwise your child loses the

connection between the correct answer and the
positive reinforcement.

e. Whatever reward you use, it should bring you and
your child together. It should be an expression of
love. Your child will want more. Every child's
greatest desire is the desire to be loved.

f. Initial simple rewards open the door for your child
to experience intrinsic satisfaction from making wise
decisions and feeling good about himself for doing
so.

g. The more your child becomes intrinsically motivated
to make wise decisions for himself, the less there is
need for any extrinsic rewards.

h. In this way the rewards pave the way for the case
method miracle, your child wanting—on his own—
to make wise decisions.

i. Checkpoint: You know it is working when your child
comes to you to tell him case stories.

5. The <u>takeaways</u>: Let it go or discuss.

After all is said and done, you can take the opportunity to
bring home any lessons learned or discuss the issues still
remaining about the case. Consider the following:

a. Use your judgment to let it go or discuss, you know
your child.

b. To leave it be is a good choice, especially in cases
describing situations similar to where your child had
made an unwise decision. Being left to think about it
in quietness allows for self-reflection, a key element
of the case method miracle.

c. There may be an opening for a teaching moment.
You can use the time to elaborate and then
summarize the principle you are trying to instill.

d. Grab any chance to answer questions your child has,
things still puzzling him about the case or the
decision.

Through the process, do your best to promote an encouraging learning environment. It is easy when you retell your child's wise decision as a case story, affirming his right choice. But when your child has done something wrong, how you proceed is a delicate matter. You have at least two options.

First, you could tell the situation as it unraveled but make the case story character choose wisely. Your child will add it up, realizing he did not go that route. Again, you do not need to say it to him, let him think about it.

Second alternative is to present the case story and the bad decision as it happened in your child's experience. You ask your child if the little boy in the story made a wise or unwise decision. Your child knows it was an unwise decision. Then you praise him for *knowing* the right answer, with perhaps an added, "I know you know how to make wise decisions." You are setting him up to right the next time. You affirm your child he has what it takes. It is supportive to him. At this point your wise course of action is probably to let it go. You give your child the space and the quiet to reflect. This is the hardest part. The tendency is to jump in pre-maturely before the powerful self-examination, self-regulation, and finally, self-accountability, to kick in within your child. Consider the case method as an alternative to timeouts and public humiliation.

18. Ground Rules—What to Mind

The following ten rules are my top guidelines to keep in mind when doing cases with children. I have included a printable card on my website, www.casemethodmiracle.com.

1. Keep it <u>simple</u>: Characters, story, decision, and rewards.

2. Make the story <u>short</u>, do not drag on and lose focus.

3. Be <u>clear</u>, no need for background or big words. Jump straight in!

4. Speak from the <u>child's viewpoint</u>, not yours.

5. Create distance from an emotionally-charged situation.

6. Enable <u>quick wins</u>, build incrementally.

7. Engineer your approach with <u>trial and error</u>.

8. <u>Save the child's face</u>, avoid public humiliation.

9. No finger pointing from the parent.

10. Give a reward right away.

III.

Case Story Examples: Jumpstarting Your Storytelling

Straight thinking leads to straight living.
Socrates

We are what we repeatedly do.
Excellence, then, is not an act, but a habit.
Aristotle

19. How to Use the Case Story Examples

The purpose is to get you started on your own

In this section of the book, I have included examples of case stories for children. The case stories I have shared attempt to describe some experiences preschool and elementary age children face. Some of these scenarios are from my family. I adapted others from my friends' experiences.

These case story examples illustrate the points I have made earlier in the book. They include how the cases are short and simple, from everyday life, and how they highlight a principle.

Pay attention to the mechanism, less to the content. The content is personal and you may disagree with some of the ideas contained in my case examples. Keep moving along to see how the mechanism works so you can adopt the approach. The purpose of these examples is to get you started with your own case storytelling by giving you examples to follow and helping you realize how simple and easy this approach is to implement.

You can use this section of the book as a story book you read to your child—and you can use the cases as they are, or you can modify them. If your child is past elementary school, my examples may not work so well. You can still read them to your child to get the idea. Alternatively, you can read them on your own to help you get started with your own case stories, cases more pertinent to your child.

If you disagree with what a case story suggests as a wise choice or with the principle or behavior advocated in the case, please skip the pages or alter the case to support your parenting principles.

For consistency, I have used a little boy as the case protagonist in all the case stories in this section. You can change the case protagonist to anyone your child may prefer. Also, I have used the first person perspective for consistency, even when the cases were from somebody else's experience.

How the example cases are laid out

Each case example in this section is contained in two pages on a spread. The parent page, on the left, is intended for parents as background material, while the child page, on the right, includes the case story and the decision-forcing question at the end of the story.

On the parent pages, I have shared some background on the case situation, the big idea behind the case, caveats, and possible follow-up questions. The purpose of the parent commentary page is to help you see a way to come up with case stories from observing your child, and how to build this kind of storytelling into your relationship with your child.

The child page is laid out to be read to your child like a story with a question in the end. You could go through the case story examples by only reading the case stories, the child pages, and not concern about the parent pages.

The goal: "I can do it!"

If, after reading through a few of the case examples, you start thinking, "This is ridiculously simple," "Anyone can do this," or, "There is nothing new about this," then I have accomplished my goal.

My goal is to show you how you can use something so basic, like storytelling, and combine it with a powerful, proven teaching method, such as the case method, to make a miracle happen. I hope the case examples encourage you to start using this approach with your child, spending one-on-one time with him.

20. Cases on Chores

Category: Chores
Case 1: Cleaning up after play

Background: The responsibility of putting toys back after playing is a regular battle in our home. Jupiter plays and often leaves toys all over the floor. Many times he does not even notice doing it, other times he wants to keep the play setup so he can continue playing the next day. I want Jupiter to learn to keep his place neat and to take care of his property, starting with putting his toys to their designated places.

Big Idea: Responsibility, I take care of whatever is mine. I am responsible. A place for everything and everything in its place. We keep things in order at our house.

Caveats: Progress, not perfection, is the name of the game with cleaning up. I often ask Jupiter to do this when there is time pressure, such as when we are heading out the door in a hurry or right before friends are coming over. It is a bad idea to transition into a case story in such a hurried situation. Perhaps a good idea is to say, "Hey, let's clean up," and then lead your child by helping him, with a supportive attitude. As the situation has passed and emotions calmed, it is a more opportune time to tell a case story about a little boy who decided to clean up.

Follow-up Questions: How do you think the little boy felt when Daddy came home and Mommy asked if he had cleaned up is toys? Do you think this boy was taking care of his toys responsibly? Would you give this little boy more toys or less toys?

Case Story: Once there was a little boy. He had lots of toys and loved to play. His favorite was to play with his planes and rocket ships. He set up his play on the floor. There was a runway for the planes and a rocket launching site from top of a sofa cushion. He also had a box he used as a hangar to keep his planes.

The little boy was in the middle of his play when Mommy walked into the room and said, "Daddy will be home in ten minutes, and we want to be ready to have dinner then. Will you please finish your play and get cleaned up?"

The little boy did not know exactly how long ten minutes was, but he knew it was a short time. Whenever Mommy came to tell him Daddy was on his way home, he would be home quickly. The little boy wanted to continue playing. He was having so much fun. He knew he had to clean up. He did not want to because he wanted to play with the same toys the next day. He looked around. He decided to put all the toys back to where they belonged.

Question: Did this little boy make a wise or unwise decision?

Category: Chores
Case 2: Leaving a mess after play

Background: Sometimes children leave a mess because they deliberately avoid cleaning up, but often they simply get carried away with another activity. The thought to clean up is the last one in their minds. The sole purpose of this case is to demonstrate how easily we forget to clean up. My idea is to show how being mindful helps us to remember our responsibilities.

Big Idea: To pay attention, to think, and to be mindful. We can learn to be responsible.

Caveats: It is easy for your child to miss the unwise action in this case. If he misses it, you might want to tell the case story again, highlighting with your voice the rule about cleaning up. When you get to the point in the story where the little boy rushes off, you make a face, an astonished, "Oh, no!" kind of look. Or simply encourage your child to listen carefully to what happens in the story.

Follow-up Questions: What should he have done? Why do you think he forgot? Was he paying attention? Was he mindful? What do you think would help him to be responsible?

Case Story: Listen to this story about a little boy. They had a rule in his house to put toys back to where they belong after playing with them. This little boy was playing with his *Star Wars* characters, his favorite toys. He knew his mommy was going to take him to play at a friend's house a little later.

Soon his mommy called out, "It is time to go! Let's get ready!" The little boy was excited. He couldn't wait to play with his friend. He rushed out from the play area, threw the *Star Wars* characters to the side, and grabbed his shoes.

Question: Did the little boy make a wise or an unwise decision?

Category: Chores
Case 3: Making bed for the first time

Background: I believe making your own bed is a routine best learned young, perhaps at two or three. The younger the better. I simplified the bed-making process so there were only two steps for my three-year-old, to straighten the pillows and pull the blanket evenly over the bed. That way it was easy to make it a routine. I decided to tell a case story about a similar bed-making process, a process that only requires two steps.

Big Idea: Responsibility for what belongs to you. Taking charge of your morning routines.

Caveats: I told this case story before I asked Jupiter to make his own bed. After I had told him the story, I did what the mommy did in the case. I showed him how to do it first, then helped him, then asked if he could do it, and finally, when he tried to do it, I offered to help.

Follow-up Questions: Whose job do you think it is to make mommy and daddy's bed after they wake up? What about you? Whose job do you think it is to make your bed?

Cases on Chores

Case Story: Let me tell you about a little boy. He had his own bedroom. He loved his room. When he was a baby, he had slept in a crib, but now he was sleeping in a big boy bed. He could get in and out of it all by himself.

One day, his mommy showed him how to make his bed. Mommy showed him how to put the pillow straight at the top end of the bed, then how to straighten the blanket and pull it over the entire bed.

Now Mommy asked the little boy to mess up the bed, as if he had slept on it. He did. That was fun. Then Mommy asked the little boy to help her make the bed. The little boy and Mommy made the bed together. It was easy. Pillow straight at the top end, then pull the blanket evenly on the bed. Mommy also showed how you have to go around the bed to pull the blanket down properly. The little boy knew how to do it now.

Finally, Mommy asked the little boy if he could mess it up one more time and show her how to make the bed all by himself. The little boy messed up the bed and then made it all by himself. Mommy hugged him and said, "You are a big boy! You can make your own bed!" Then she said it would be the little boy's job every morning to make his own bed. The little boy was proud of his new chore.

The next morning when Mommy came to wake him up, the little boy woke up and remembered about making his own bed. Mommy said she can help, but the little boy said, "Mommy, I can do it all by myself." He did.

Question: Did the little boy make a wise or an unwise decision?

21. Cases on Bedtime Challenges

Category: Bedtime
Case 4: Chimes makes bath time

Background: We have challenges with bedtime routines. Until I made the call for bath time to originate from an agreed-upon outside source instead of me, starting the bedtime routines was more or less a fight. I told Jupiter the case story before executing the chiming, hoping Jupiter would then suggest the idea for himself. He did. He simply asked me if I had a phone like the one in the story. I proceeded to show him a few options for the chimes and let him pick one. He did.

Big Idea: Schedule and routines help us. We have to get enough sleep to wake up ready to go.

Caveats: After I introduced this way of starting the bedtime routines, I would tell Jupiter a case like this while he was in the bath, with the wise decision made in the end, just like Jupiter had done, to help him see how he was making wise decisions.

Follow-up Questions: Do you think it was hard or easy for the little boy to stop his play and start his bath instead? Do you think he wanted to keep playing? Who made the decision to go take a bath?

Case Story: Once there was a little boy whose mommy had a phone with a chime to tell them when it was time to take a bath. The chime went like this: "Baappappaa, Baappappaa." The little boy knew that when the chime went off it was time to take a bath no matter what they were doing.

One evening his mommy and daddy were cleaning up after dinner, and the little boy was just about to start playing with his blocks when the chime went off. He knew what it meant. He wanted to tell his mommy. He went to his mommy and said: "Mommy, it is bath time!" He then put the blocks back in the toy box and headed for the bathroom with his mommy.

Question: Was that a wise or unwise decision?

Category: Bedtime
Case 5: Listening to a story

Background: Jupiter loves me to read to him. However, there are times he gets excited about something else and pays no attention to my reading. Most of the time I am all right with it, and we diverge. However, when we are preparing to go to bed, I expect him to slow down his energy level and be present to the story. So, at bedtime when I read to him and Jupiter engages in something else, I pause and address the situation. However, I also want him to start taking charge of it, not just responding to my requests of paying attention. The case method worked well to push the ownership of his behavior on him.

Big Idea: Being present and mindful. Bedtime is not playtime.

Caveats: Paying attention and staying focused is developmental. It may be inappropriate to expect obedience in this area if the child is developmentally immature. Also, I know in many families children are allowed to play or do other activities while listening to a story. They are already multitasking as a toddler. Finally, an older child may even be expected to ask questions and engage in a dialogue about the story during the reading time. These scenarios call for different case stories.

Follow-up Questions: Was the little boy able to answer if he liked the story? Why? What do you think would have been a wise thing to do while Mommy was reading the story?

Case Story: Once there was a little boy. He loved playing in his playroom. Even more than playing he loved listening to his mommy read stories to him.

It was the evening, and Mommy was about to read some stories before the little boy went to sleep. Mommy had a new book. It was his favorite series about little bears. The little boy was excited. They sat on the sofa right next to his bed. Mommy started reading. The little boy was so excited he had a hard time sitting still. He started climbing up and down the sofa, playing with the pillows. It was fun. He got down from the sofa and fetched a teddy bear to play with it. Mommy kept reading the story. Then she finished. She asked, "Did you like that story?" The little boy had no idea. He had been playing, not listening.

Question: Did the little boy make a wise or unwise decision?

22. Cases on Obedience

Category: Obedience
Case 6: Setting the table for dinner with a bad attitude

Background: When Jupiter had just turned three, we started asking him to contribute to the household duties. I explained to him it was important for all members of the family to participate. Setting the table before dinner was one of the first chores for him. I quickly realized it was an opportunity to teach him three facets of obedience I deemed important. Those three facets include that when we obey, we have to do it all the way, right away, and with a good attitude. If the facets—or any of them—were absent while accomplishing the task, then full obedience was questioned. The case stories were focused on Jupiter recognizing whether the three aspects were present when the little boy in the case obeyed and accomplished his chore.

    Big Idea: Obedience is incomplete obedience unless we do it right away, all the way, and with a good attitude. However, giving yourself and others grace is as important.

    Caveats: In our family Jupiter gets credit and praise for setting the table even when he does not fully obey per the definition. It has been an opportunity for Jupiter to learn about grace. It is tricky. I want to avoid being legalistic and overly demanding while still teaching a clear standard. I believe in helping Jupiter to aspire towards a set standard without feeling himself a failure when he does not perfectly achieve it. Grace fills the gap. Sometimes I complete my responsibilities with a bad attitude, too, but at least the tasks get done. I give myself grace and learn from the experience to have a better attitude next time.

    Follow-up Questions: Which did he do? What did he miss? Did he have a good attitude?

Cases on Obedience

Case Story: Once there was a little boy. His mommy had taught him that when we obey, we have to do three things. Three things. Whatever we do, we have to do it right away, all the way, and with a good attitude. Otherwise it is not full obedience. This little boy loved Mommy and wanted to learn to obey.

One of the little boy's chores was to set the table while Mommy was preparing dinner. Sometimes Mommy let him watch his favorite program on television while she was cooking.

One night, the little boy was watching his program when Mommy came to tell him it was time to set the table. The little boy jumped up, "But I am still watching!" He was upset because he would have rather continued watching the program.

Mommy went back to the kitchen. The little boy knew it was his job to set the table. He was upset about it. He wanted to watch television. He paused and made a decision. He turned off the television, went to the kitchen, and set the table. He put the plates, the glasses, and the forks and knives on the right places. He finished every piece onto the table. He said to Mommy loudly, "Done!" He stomped off to his room.

Question: Did he obey all the way, right away, and with a good attitude?

Category: Obedience
Case 7: Setting the table for dinner haphazardly

Background: In this story I have changed one of the three points of obedience I discussed in the prior case story. It is the same case story as on the previous page, but the boy now obeys in a different way. The boy has a good attitude and starts on the chore right away, but he does not finish his job. Keeping the story mostly the same and changing one of the three aspects of obedience helps to illustrate how to pay attention to predefined criteria and listen carefully.

Big Idea: Obedience is incomplete unless we do it right away, all the way, and with a good attitude. However, giving yourself and others grace is as important.

Caveats: Right before I have the point in the story where the little boy chooses to do the unwise action, I sometimes interject "listen carefully now" into the storytelling. It helps small children to focus and pay attention. Jupiter has to think about several aspects of an activity. I have witnessed this kind of awareness practice to pave way to disciplined behavior, something I value.

Follow-up Questions: Which two of the three things did he do? Which did the little boy miss? What do you think happened? Do you think the little boy's mommy was happy about him helping her even though he did not do all of the three things required for full obedience? The answer to this question in our family is a "yes."

Cases on Obedience

Case Story: There was a little boy. His mommy had taught him that when we obey, we have to do three things. Three things. Whatever we do, we have to do it right away, all the way, and with a good attitude. Otherwise it is not full obedience. This little boy loved his mommy and wanted to learn to obey.

One of his chores was to set the table while Mommy was preparing the dinner. Sometimes Mommy let the little boy watch his favorite program on television while she was cooking. One night the little boy was watching his television program when Mommy came to tell him it was time to set the table.

The little boy jumped up, "Yes, Mommy!" He turned off the program and started setting the table. He first put the plates on the table, then the cups, and the potholders. But right in the middle of setting the table, he noticed one of his toy cars on the floor. He started playing with it. He forgot about setting the table. He forgot about putting the forks and the knives on the table setting.

Question: Did he obey all the way, right away, and with a good attitude?

Category: Obedience
Case 8: Setting the table for dinner after being asked several times

Background: This is a third variation of the original table setting case. In addition to the three points of obedience, this case story gave us a chance to talk about how we can use our words to communicate our thoughts. The little boy in the case said "Yes, Mommy," but did not follow through. He partially ignored the request even though he verbally agreed. Instead, he could have asked his mommy if it was all right for him to finish watching the episode and then come set the table.

Big Idea: Obedience is incomplete obedience unless we do it right away, all the way, and with a good attitude. Listening carefully and being able to judge an act based on a predefined criteria. Using our words to express disagreement or suggest another option to accomplish the same task.

Caveats: I think using the same case story setup with a slight variation helps to bring home the related points. Giving Jupiter examples how I may express disagreement and another solution shows him it is all right to disagree and how he might do that.

Follow-up Questions: Which of the three things did he do? What could he have said to his mommy? Maybe, ask his mommy if he could finish that episode and then set the table?

Case Story: So this little boy, again, was watching his favorite television program while Mommy was preparing dinner. He loved the program. He also knew it was his job to set the table.

When Mommy came to tell him it was time to set the table, the little boy said: "Yes, Mommy." He loved Mommy. He knew it was his responsibility to set the table, but he wanted to finish the episode he was watching. He did not say anything else to his mommy. He continued watching. When the episode ended, the next one started, and the little boy had forgotten all about setting the table.

Mommy came back. She said: "Soon we will be ready to eat, will you please set the table?" "Yes, Mommy," the little boy responded happily. He realized he had forgotten all about it. He turned off the program. He went to the kitchen and hummed along as he carefully put every piece to the table. The table was beautifully set when Daddy came home, and it was time to eat.

Question: Did he obey all the way, right away, and with a good attitude?

Category: Obedience
Case 9: Setting the table for dinner with full obedience

Background: In this final version of the table setting case, I am painting a picture of full obedience. I highlight how the process runs smoothly and everyone is happy. I want to show how there is pleasantness all around when we pay attention to each other and communicate respect with what we do and how we do it.

Big Idea: Learning what full obedience is and how obeying parents leads to pleasantness all around.

Caveats: This is where I do super tickles and hugs to show excitement about such full obedience. I praise Jupiter for knowing the answers in the other cases, I just show extra excitement for the little boy as he did all three. It is hard to do all three, for all of us.

Follow-up Questions: How do you think the little boy felt after he had set the table?

Case Story: Again, this little boy was watching his favorite television program while Mommy was preparing dinner. He loved the program. He also knew it was his job to set the table.

When Mommy came to tell him it was time to set the table, the little boy responded: "Yes, Mommy." He loved Mommy. He knew it was his responsibility to set the table, and he wanted to do it. The little boy turned off the program and exclaimed, smiling, "I love you, Mommy!"

The little boy went to the kitchen and hummed along as he carefully put every piece on the table. Plates and potholders, then the glasses, the forks, the knives, and the napkins. The table was beautifully set when Daddy came home, and it was time to eat. Mommy was happy with what the little boy had accomplished. Daddy even commented about how nice the table looked.

Question: Did he obey all the way, right away, and with a good attitude?

23. Cases on Telling the Truth

Category: Telling the truth
Case 10: Washing hands

Background: I started advocating for telling the truth early. I connected it with building trust. Once we lie to someone, how can they ever know whether we are telling the truth? In case stories, I used everyday scenarios where it is tempting to lie. Washing hands is a simple event where lying is easy and seems inconsequential. If Jupiter learns to stand firm and do the right thing even when nobody is looking, it is a step towards being accountable to self for honesty.

Big Idea: Tell the truth. Honesty paves way to integrity.

Caveats: This is the perfect case to make an "Oh, no!" face when the little boy decides to lie. It is easy to change this case story to where the little boy washes his hands properly, and when his mother asks about it he can answer affirmatively with a clear conscience. Alternatively, you can change the story such that the little boy does not wash his hands properly but when his mother asks about it, he tells the truth.

It is tempting for children to lie to please a parent. Cases like this help show children that parents like honesty better than covering up to please them. I admit this example has two decisions the boy made, to wash his hands properly *and* to tell the truth. It is inconsistent with my rules about how to build case stories. The main focus is the decision to tell the truth about washing hands.

Follow-up Questions: How easy is it to just rinse your hands quickly without soap and tell your parents have done the job properly even if you didn't? Do you think it matters?

Case Story: Every time before a meal this little boy was to wash his hands. Mommy had showed him how to use the soap and rub it on his hands, top, bottom, and in between the fingers. Just holding his hands under running water would leave invisible germs on his hands. Therefore, using soap was necessary. Sometimes the little boy had to wash his hands even when they felt clean.

One evening he had been playing inside with his toys when Mommy asked him to wash his hands before dinner. The little boy thought his hands were clean. He had only been playing inside, not in the dirt outside. He went to the bathroom, turned on the water, and let it run through his fingers. Did he really need to use soap? He decided to skip it. There was no need for it. His hands were quite clean. He finished rinsing and dried his hands on a towel.

Question 1: Was that a wise or an unwise decision?

When he sat at the dinner table, Mommy asked, "Did you wash your hands properly?" "Yes, Mommy," the little boy answered.

Question 2: Did the little boy make a wise or an unwise decision?

Category: Telling the truth
Case 11: Accepting candy when not allowed, then lying about it

Background: Saturdays are the only days we eat candy in our family. It makes it easy at the grocery store and at other popup situations during the week. Keeping away from candies during the week grows self-discipline and honesty in small steps. Each "No, thank you" is a small expression to say, yet a huge step towards discipline. They are also usually black and white situations. You either take it or you do not. It is hard to half-eat a piece of candy.

Big Idea: Tell the truth. It is a bad idea to be dishonest, hiding behind a lie.

Caveats: If you find this too strict to share with your child, skip it, just like you would any other of my examples you do not like. I am sharing it as an example of how you take something you have instituted in your family as "this is how we do it" and make up a case story about it.

The idea that doing something wrong is all right as long as nobody knows about it will tempt children at early age, shortly after they learn to talk and interact with others. Also, all children lie, some more than others. I believe in addressing the issue earlier rather than later. This kind of a case will prepare your child at least to stop and think—to be mindful—when he is faced with a temptation to tell a lie.

Follow-up Questions: How do you think the little boy felt when he lied about not having had a snack and that they had just played? Do you think it would have been hard for the little boy not to take his favorite candy? What do you think would have helped him to refuse the candy?

Case Story: Listen, let me tell you about this little boy. Saturdays were special for him. They were his candy days. His parents let him pick a bag of candy. However, they had agreed that to get the bag of candy on Saturdays, he would refuse candies on other days, except on special occasions such as a birthday party. The little boy loved candy days.

One day he was playing at his friend's house. His friend was snacking on gummy bears. He offered the little boy a piece. The little boy stopped to think. "Would it really hurt so much if I just take one?" he thought. He did not have to tell Mommy anything. He could just tell Mommy that they had played, nothing about eating a piece of candy. He took the gummy bear and said, "Thank you!"

When Mommy came to pick him up, she asked, "Did you have fun? What did you guys do? Did you have a snack?" "We just played," the little boy replied, not mentioning anything about the candy. He did not want to disappoint Mommy.

Question: Was that a wise or unwise decision? Or maybe he made two decisions?

Category: Telling the truth
Case 12: Doing a wrong and covering it up

Background: If we lie, we often try to cover it up so
nobody would find out. The children do the same thing. It is
wrong. In a simpler case, we recognize the telling of the lie
as the unwise decision. I wanted to make it even worse by
adding the cover up to the case story. Unwise to lie and
unwise to cover it up.

Big Idea: Telling a lie is wrong.

Caveats: Another case that gives opportunities to make
"Oh, no!" faces to highlight the bad decisions the little boy
makes. After reading this case, you could stop in the middle
and make the little boy in the story affirm his standing to
refuse the candy. It would be the wise decision. If I tell two
cases that are almost the same back to back, I often say,
"Listen to this one, it is almost like the one I just told you,"
or something along those lines to prepare Jupiter for a
repeat version of the previous story.

Follow-up Questions: What would have been the wise
choice? Could he still do the wise choice after they hid the
wrappers? How? If you can cover up your bad deed, does it
make it all right? If your friend does the wrong decision,
does that make it right for you?

Cases on Telling the Truth

Case Story: Once there was a little boy. His friend had
come to play with him at his house. The friend noticed a jar
of wrapped chocolate candies on the kitchen counter. He
asked the little boy, "Can we have some?" The little boy
answered, "No, Mommy bought them for our movie night
tomorrow." The friend continued, "Let's just take one each,
it will be okay. Your mommy will not even notice."

The little boy was uncomfortable. But he wanted to be
nice to his friend and give him what he wanted. He also
wanted to taste them. The two got the jar out and picked a
chocolate each. They were delicious.

Question: Was it a wise or unwise decision to eat that
candy?

Let's continue the story. Now there was a problem with
the wrapping paper. If they put them in the trash, Mommy
would probably see the wraps and know they had taken the
chocolates. "Let's hide the wraps," the friend suggested. The
boys stuffed the wrappers through the air conditioning vent.

When Mommy came from upstairs to check on the boys,
she noticed the candy jar on the kitchen counter without its
top on. The little boy saw it, too. "Did you boys take some
movie night candies?" Mommy inquired. The little boy
shook his head. The friend replied, "No, Ma'am, we did
not."

Question: Was it a wise or unwise decision to cover up
the unwise decision by hiding the candy wraps? And how
about denying having taken any?

Category: Telling the truth
Case 13: Keeping a promise

Background: Some lies are easily found out, some may never be found out. Some lies are serious, some inconsequential. I wanted to introduce the emerging grey areas to my four-year-old. At this age children know how to lie and some even how to lie well. I wanted to get Jupiter thinking about whether a lie is less of a lie when it does not hurt anyone or when nobody else would ever even know about it.

Big Idea: Honesty to yourself is as important as honesty to others.

Caveats: This case can be easily modified to have the little boy watch another episode and nobody ever knowing about it. In the story, the boy's dad is unaware how long one episode lasts, and since he is immersed in his work, he probably would not notice whether the boy was watching fifteen minutes or an hour.

However, when the child withholds the truth or tells a lie nobody will ever know about, is it true that nobody ever knows about it when *he* does? Isn't that the worst, to live in a lie? The simpler the case, the clearer the principle will come to bear for your child.

Follow-up Questions: Do you think the daddy in the story would know if the little boy watched two episodes instead of one? If he would not even know the difference, then would it be all right to do it? Why? Why not? How do you think the little boy would feel telling the lie? Do you think he would think about it again later? What if he went to tell his daddy he had finished and asked if he could watch one more episode? Would that be honest? Do you think the daddy may be alright with it?

Cases on Telling the Truth

Case Story: This little boy was spending an evening with his daddy while his mommy had to attend an event. The little boy wanted to watch his favorite program since Daddy had to do some work before he could play. The little boy loved doing puzzles with Daddy when they were together, but since Daddy had to work the little boy wanted to watch television. Daddy said the little boy could watch one episode of his favorite program. Once he was finished with the episode, he should come tell him, so Daddy could wrap up his work. Then they could start on the puzzles.

The little boy started the episode about a little tiger. When the episode finished, the little boy remembered his promise. He had promised to tell Daddy he was done with the episode. But he wanted to watch another one. Daddy was still working. The little boy paused. He recalled he had told Daddy he would go and let him know when he was finished. However, Daddy would never know whether he watched one or two episodes. Daddy did not know how long an episode was. Yet the little boy knew Daddy would ask him something about it, and then he would have to lie. He did not want to lie. He called out, "Daddy, I finished the first episode! Can we do the puzzles now?"

Question: Do you think the little boy made a wise or unwise decision?

24. Cases on Playground Events

Category: Playground Events
Case 14: Introducing yourself

Background: Children love playing with each other, and often do so seamlessly, integrating into someone else's play. I wanted Jupiter to understand the common courtesy of introducing himself before jumping into play. I have told this case several times in slightly different circumstances.

Big Idea: Introducing yourself is good manners and shows respect. It makes conversation simpler for everyone. We should do it automatically.

Caveats: For a long time Jupiter continued jumping in to play with other children without introducing himself. I decided to let it go even though I knew he knew how to introduce himself. I wanted him to own his choice. Based on the case stories, he knew the right thing to do. It took a few months before Jupiter started sating his name and asking for the other child's name. It may work the best to give our children time before holding them accountable. It took time for Jupiter to process and own the wise choice. I felt that if I pushed it on him too aggressively, I was telling him what to do. That would not affect the case method miracle. The case method miracle works when the child starts owning the choice—and that might take time with failures along on the path.

Follow-up Questions: Does your name matter to you? Do you think it matters to others? How does it make you feel when someone asks for your name?

Case Story: Listen carefully to this story. A little boy went to the playground with Mommy. When the little boy and his mommy arrived at the playground, the little boy saw a little girl climbing on the monkey bars. The little boy loved climbing on the monkey bars. He had not seen the girl before, but she looked about his age. She was having a good time and smiling. The little boy wanted to play with her. He went up to her and said, "Hi, my name is John. What is your name? Do you want to play?"

Question: Was that a wise or unwise decision?

Category: Playground Events
Case 15: Refusing to climb trees when not allowed

Background: On the side of a playground near our house, there were young trees. They were not strong enough for climbing, nor were the branches strong enough for pulling down. I had been watching children playing and hurting the small trees by pulling down the branches. The branches would snap. I knew Jupiter would be tempted to go along at some point. I wanted to help him picture a situation where other children are doing something that he knows is unwise and then have to make a decision for himself. I made up a case about it.

Big Idea: Knowing and doing the right thing even when it is hard.

Caveats: I was sure to include in the case the escape. The escape was to focus on something else, run off to play with the playground equipment. I try to repeat the idea to my son that when he is tempted to do something wrong, the wise choice is to get away from the situation if possible. It is better to focus on a constructive activity. The rest of the playground would provide an easy escape for him, to go do something else.

Follow-up Questions: Do you think the little boy wanted to play in the trees? Was it hard or easy to say and do what he did? Why? What did he do next? Did that help him?

Case Story: Once there was a little boy. He loved going to the playgrounds. He was at a playground with Mommy. There was a group of small trees on the side of the playground. Mommy had told the little boy not to hang on the branches or climb those trees because they were too weak. They would break and die. The little boy was playing with three other boys around the little trees. One of the boys started breaking off branches from one of the little trees to use as a stick sword. Then that same boy tried to hang on one of the branches, saying, "Let's play in the trees!"

Our little boy remembered these trees were too weak, that they would break and then die. They were young trees not strong enough for climbing. The little boy stood tall and said, "That is an unwise decision. Those trees are not strong enough to climb. They will break." Then the little boy decided to run off and play at the playground equipment.

Question: Was that a wise or unwise decision?

Category: Playground Events
Case 16: Toy grab

Background: At public play places toys are shared. Toy grabbing is commonplace. I knew we had to establish a process to handle it. I have advocated for simply "letting it go" if someone come and grabs a toy from my child. However, it is a different story if your child is playing with siblings with a clear, shared rule about not taking someone else's toy when he is still playing with it. This case can easily be altered to address playing at home with a sibling. Would the wise choice then be different if a clearly established rule was broken? Perhaps then it is an opportunity for the little boy to stand up for what is right and express it in words.

Big Idea: Forgiveness. Playing with friends and learning to let go of arguments. Answering a wrong with a right.

Caveats: Instead of telling cases about doing wrong, I often tell a story about a wise little boy first. I let that sink in while I embrace Jupiter for recognizing the wise decision. Shortly after, I tell the case story but now make the little boy respond unwisely, perhaps he runs after the other child and snatches the toy truck back in anger. Perhaps he even hits the other child in addition to taking the truck back. Maybe he uses ugly words. Helping Jupiter look at those behaviors as an outsider who has been embraced for knowing the wise choice seems to help him to identify more strongly with the wise approach.

Follow-up Questions: Do you think it was easy for the little boy to just let it go and start playing something else? What do you think he thought about doing when he was angry? Would that have been wise? What was the wise decision when the girl snatched his truck without even asking?

Case Story: This little boy was at an indoor playground. He loved playing in the toddler area. They had trucks, cars, and trains with which to play. A particular truck was his favorite. It looked just like the dump truck in a storybook he had at home. The little boy saw the truck and ran to seize it. He started playing. He put blocks on the dumper and turned around to pick some more blocks. When he turned back to the truck, a little girl had grabbed it. She ran off to play with it. The little boy felt sad. He had loved playing with the truck and had only just began his play. The little girl had not even asked for her turn. She had just taken it. The little boy felt angry. He wanted to finish playing with it.

The little boy sighed and looked around. There were other toys. He would not let it ruin his day. He could play with the truck another time. He noticed a train and two train cars lying around and decided to play with them.

Question: Was that a wise or unwise decision?

Category: Playground Events
Case 17: Using words when a friend is ugly

Background: I had seen something similar to this case scenario with my son. Jupiter had simply frozen when another child was ugly to him. I wanted to show him a wise way to approach it, to use his words. When someone is ugly to us it hurts. It is hard to stay calm, address the hurtful words, and walk away.

Since I have been trying to teach Jupiter to use his words, I wanted to give an example of how to do it in this kind of a situation. I talked to him about how we feel better about such an attack after we have expressed the wrong the other person did to us, even if the other person refuses to say he is sorry. Doing our part is the most important thing. It is better to focus on what my part is instead of the other person's wrong. This simple case, half-a-minute long, allowed me to advocate for using words and thus empowering instead of becoming a victim.

Big Idea: Standing up for what is right by using our words to confront a wrong, even when we feel hurt.

Caveats: If you would rather promote another type of response, try changing the little boy's response in this case story to what you would recommend as the wise decision. You could also make this a serial case story by extending it with what happened next. Then you would ask your child at each decision point whether the little boy's choice was wise or unwise.

Follow-up Questions: How do you think the little boy felt afterwards? Was he still hurt? Do you think he felt better? What could he do next? Go play with something else?

Case Story: Once there was a little boy. He had a friend with whom he loved to play. They were best friends. One day they were playing together, and the friend said to the little boy, "I never want to play with you for the rest of my life. I am going to press this button, and it is going to make you explode." The little boy just looked at his friend. He felt hurt. A tear came to his eye. Then he said, "That is not a nice thing to say. Friends do not hurt each other. Friends care about each other."

Question: Did the little boy make a wise or unwise decision?

Category: Playground Events
Case 18: Running to Mommy when a friend is ugly

Background: This is almost the same case story as the previous one, but now the little boy acts like a victim and runs from the issue to be consoled. It is common behavior for a two- or three-year old. However, once Jupiter had learnt to say a few words, I felt he was capable to start handling these kinds of situations. I wanted to encourage him to share with me what he had experienced, but only after he had managed it properly, taken the first steps he could take.

This case shows a contrast to the prior case where the little boy used his words. Here, the little boy is letting the hurt feelings take over, running away from the situation to be comforted.

Big Idea: Do not run away from problem situations.

Caveats: Depending on how you as a parent or caregiver believe about handling situations when someone comes and says something ugly to you, the case can easily be built to model that response. When you keep it simple, it helps your child to identify the desired choice.

Follow-up Questions: Since the little boy made an unwise choice, you could ask probing questions to help your child express the wise approach on his own. Instead of running to Mommy, what could the little boy have done?

You could also take the previous case and this one, telling your child, "Now, think about the little boy who said to the friend that what he said was not a nice thing to say, let's call that little boy, Boy A. Let's call this little boy, the one running to Mommy, Boy B. Which one, Boy A or Boy B, do you think made a wise decision? Why? Which boy would you like to be?

Case Story: Once ether was a little boy. He had a friend with whom he loved to play. They were best friends. One day, they were playing together, and the friend said to the little boy, "I never want to play with you for the rest of my life. I am going to press this button, and it is going to make you explode!" The little boy just looked at his friend. He felt hurt. A tear came to his eye. He ran to Mommy, crying.

Question: Was that a wise or unwise decision?

Category: Playground Events
Case 19: A friend forgot his light saber, sharing

Background: My position on sharing toys is to advocate being responsible for one's toys. It means taking care of them by keeping them where they belong, taking good care of them, and only sharing them with friends who know how to play with them. These aspects of sharing give ideas for a few cases where a little boy has to decide if it is wise to share his toy.

Big Idea: Share responsibly. It is all right to share your toys with friends you know are responsible with them.

Caveats: Calling the friend a best friend in this case implies the little boy knows him well and has played with him before. This best friend is responsible and handles toys with care, not breaking everything he touches. You could retell this case by changing the best friend into a friend. You can describe the friend as someone who is fun to play with but who breaks everything he touches. In that case, it would be an unwise decision to share the sword. A wise choice might be to suggest another play, without the light sabers.

Follow-up Questions: Did the little boy know his best friend well? Did he know the best friend would take a good care of his light saber?

Case Story: This little boy had a play date with his best friend. He had shared his toys with his best friend before. His best friend was always careful with his toys. They both had enjoyed learning about *Star Wars* characters and stories. They loved playing with their light saber swords. The little boy had a blue light saber, and his best friend had a green one. The little boy had been looking forward to playing with the light sabers all day.

When the little boy arrived at the playground, his best friend was already there, waiting, but had a sad look on his face. "What happened?" asked the little boy. "I forgot to bring my light saber," his best friend responded and continued, "Now we cannot play with the *Star Wars* toys."

The little boy was disappointed. Then he had an idea. They could make with just one light saber, he thought to himself. He looked at his best friend and smiled, "What if we just play with my light saber and take turns? You can take it first, I'll get a stick and pretend it is a light saber."

Question: Was that a wise or unwise decision?

Category: Playground Events
Case 20: Another child asks to play with the lightsaber

Background: Whenever Jupiter brings popular toys to the playground, someone asks to play with them. One time, he let a stranger take and play with his parachute toy. This boy was so rough with it that a piece broke off. We were not able to repair it. It taught my son to be protective of his toys by not sharing them without careful consideration. Again, using his words was important, and this case highlights the idea of expressing his desires with words.

Big Idea: You do not have to share everything you have with everyone else.

Caveats: An equally wise approach could be to say that what the little boy chose to do was unwise because he did not know this big boy. Maybe the little boy should have simply said he does not want to lend his toy. If you encourage your child to always share his toys, then sharing is a wise choice every time.

Follow-up Questions: What did the little boy know about the big boy to conclude he was responsible? Do you think that was enough?

Case Story: Once there was a little boy. He had a favorite new toy, a blue lightsaber that lit on and off from a small button on the handle. It also made the lightsaber sound. The little boy wanted to take it to the playground to play Jedi warrior. Daddy took him to the playground where the little boy started playing right away. He knew how to move and use the lightsaber. It was fun to play with the light, too.

Soon, an older boy came up and commented on his sword, "What a nice lightsaber. Can I try it?" The little boy had never played with this big boy before. However, the little boy had seen him with a small sister, taking care of her and playing with her. He seemed to be nice to the little sister. The little boy smiled and said, "Thank you. It is my favorite toy. Maybe you can try it just for a little time? It breaks easily. Can you be careful?"

Question: Was that a wise or unwise decision?

25. Cases on Table Manners

Category: Table Manners
Case 21: Polite and rude table manners

Background: This is an example of a case story with several decision points followed by a question. The format aligns well with a dinner setting where your child has to make several decisions about how to behave while eating with others.

Big Idea: Choosing proper table manners every time.

Caveats: The key to cases with serial questions is to describe the common setting up front, then ask a question pertaining to each part, followed by the next situation and the related question, then the next and so on. If you tell the full story and then ask all the questions in the end, it tends to be too overwhelming. To keep it simple, focus on one issue per question. It helps to drive home each issue.

Follow-up Questions: Once your child judges the little boy's chosen behavior, follow-up questions can help him confirm his judgment. For example, if the little boy did something rude in the case story, then the follow-up question would be what the polite thing to do would have been. Or if the little boy did something considerate and polite, then the question could be to describe what made that response polite, and how he showed consideration to others.

Cases on Table Manners

Case Story: Once there was a little boy. Please listen carefully, because you are going to evaluate his choices four times during this story.

It was dinner time. The parents, the little boy, and his sister were sitting at the dinner table. Mommy had made mashed potatoes, grilled salmon, and sautéed vegetables. There was also a bread basket on the table. Daddy asked if the children wanted water or milk. The little boy waited for his sister to reply first and then said: "Can I have milk, please."

Question 1: Was that polite or rude? How?

Once he had his drink, the little boy was ready for his favorite dish, mashed potatoes. The serving plate was a bit far from him. It was on the other side of the table. The little boy decided to stand up and reach across the table for the ladle and the bowl of mashed potatoes.

Question 2: Was that good or bad manners? Why? What do you think would have been good manners?

The little boy loved mashed potatoes but disliked the sautéed vegetables. Daddy gave him a piece of grilled salmon and said, "Let me give you some vegetables, too." The little boy looked at the vegetable pan. It looked like it was broccoli and mushrooms mixed up. He liked broccoli but disliked mushrooms. He did not want mushrooms. Daddy put a serving on his plate. It had both broccoli and mushrooms in it. The little boy cringed inside but decided not to make a fuss about it. He could eat the broccoli and show good effort with the mushrooms by eating one. He did.

Question 3: How easy do you think it was to do that? Do you think his parents were okay if he did not finish all the mushrooms since he tried one?

When the little boy was finished eating, he wanted to go play. He stood up and left the table without a word.

Question 4: Was that polite or rude? What could he have done to be polite?

Category: Table manners
Case 22: Sneaking food to sister's plate

Background: Children often come up with ways to circumvent the rules they are to follow. They want it to look like they are doing what is right even though they are not. I had witnessed this scenario, described on the next page, and I wondered what the little boy would say if I sneaked some of my food onto *his* plate.

Big Idea: Having good table manners helps us get along pleasantly. Let's remember the Golden Rule, do unto others what you would have them to do unto you.

Caveats: Most of our children have discreetly covered up something they have done wrong. Instead of continuing on that path of justifying a wrong because nobody saw it, this case gives a way to open a discussion about it. The child can evaluate the behavior of the case protagonist. Then you can discuss it. A way to do it is to start by asking, "What if I did that to *you*? Would *you* like it?"

Follow-up Questions: Why? What would have been a wiser way to handle it? Do you think the little boy could have talked to his daddy about it?

Case Story: Once there was a little boy. He was at a restaurant eating with Mommy, Daddy, and his baby sister. He liked the restaurant. Every time they went, he was excited to choose what he wanted to eat.

This time the little boy had ordered some chicken nuggets, rice, and a fruit bowl. Mommy ordered the same for the baby sister. She was a good eater and never complained. The little boy enjoyed his fruit bowl and listened to his daddy telling about the plans for going to the park the next day.

When the little boy tried his nuggets, they were cold. He tried to eat them, but he did not like them cold. He knew he should eat most of them. Daddy was eating while Mommy had to excuse herself to go to the restroom. The little boy had an idea. He grabbed some of his nuggets and sneaked them on his baby sister's plate. Daddy did not notice.

Question: Was that a wise or unwise decision?

26. Cases on Listening to Authorities

Category: Listening to authorities
Case 23: Leaving a playdate

Background: When children are playing, they often ignore their parents or caregivers who have come to tell them it is time to stop and transition to another activity. I want to teach Jupiter to respond to people when they talk to him. Ignoring a problem does not make it go away, and ignoring a person talking to you is disrespectful. I want Jupiter to at least acknowledge me when I talk to him, even if he does not have a response or cannot do anything about it at the time. The child can accomplish this with a simple "Okay" or "Yes, Mommy." If I ask my son to do something, then I expect him to agree and do it, or express his disagreement. With this case I can help him to see the wise way to do it and how it makes the situation unfold smoothly.

    Big Idea: We respond to authority. When someone talks to us, we acknowledge them and respond to them.

    Caveats: There is something interesting about teaching the child to respond, "Yes, Mommy," to a request or a comment. It bends the child's attitude towards obedience before actually obeying. I have discovered that Jupiter's positive attitude—which begins with "Yes, Mommy"—towards my requests goes a long way to obedience.

    Follow-up Questions: Do you think it would have been wise to throw a temper tantrum since he still wanted to play? Since the little boy had such good manners about leaving, do you think the nanny would be happy to take him on playdates again?

Case Story: Let me tell you about a little boy. He was on a playdate at his friend's house. His friend had fun toys and a big playroom. The friend and the little boy were having a good time playing with a new Lego set. He was not even thinking about leaving and going home. He heard his mother coming up the stairs to the playroom. She said they were going to have to get ready to leave in ten minutes. The little boy heard what his mother had said. He wanted to stay longer, the time had gone by so fast. He smiled and said, "Okay," and continued playing with his friend. Ten minutes later his mother came back to say it was time to put the toys away and leave. The little boy looked up, "All right. Time to clean up." The little boy stood up and started putting the toys away.

Question: Was that a wise or unwise decision?

Category: Listening to authorities
Case 24: Taking a phone without permission

Background: Some rules seem harmless to break. Does that make it all right to do? I have been trying to help Jupiter understand we make rules with his *and* everyone else's best interests in mind. Sometimes we may feel that following a rule is unnecessary, but it is not only ourselves we have to consider. That is the principle I have tried to get across to Jupiter. If an authority figure lays out a rule, then it is wise to follow it. If we choose to break the rule, then have to accept the consequences and might be on a slippery slope. For example, I might think, "So what if I run the red light? It is 4 a.m. in the morning. Nobody is on the road and I slowed down to check no cars are coming." What would be next? What if someone else decided to do the same thing, at the same time?

Big Idea: Parental rules are there to help and protect us.

Caveats: Learning to do the right thing even when nobody sees you is a big deal. It is when accountability for oneself shines brightest. The more I can facilitate and create opportunities for Jupiter to do this, make wise decisions for his own sake, the more he learns to stand alone for his principles and be independent.

Follow-up Questions: Do you think the little boy's mommy would find out what he did? Would that make it all right to take the phone? If he wanted to play the game on the phone, what could he have done? What do you think about going to talk to his mommy about it?

Case Story: Listen to what this little boy chose to do. He loved to play a game on his mommy's phone. However, he was not allowed to take the phone without asking his mommy first.

One evening, the little boy was working on a puzzle on the floor. He saw Mommy's phone on the table. Mommy was in another room working on the computer. The little boy wanted to take a break from the puzzle and play the game on his mommy's phone. He knew he should not take the phone without asking. But he decided he was only going to play for a little time. "Only one minute," the little boy thought to himself. He did not ask for permission. He took the phone and tapped on the game icon.

Question: Was that a wise or unwise decision?

27. Cases on Attitude Issues

Category: Attitude issues
Case 25: Handling jobs responsibly

Background: Every task accomplished bears the signature of whoever completed that job. Those children who can be trusted with small jobs, can be trusted with bigger jobs and responsibilities later. The same principle carries into adulthood. Children are often asked to do chores and one-off jobs. Learning to take full responsibility for those jobs early is monumental in learning to be responsible. I use small responsibilities at home to help Jupiter understand this principle.

    Big Idea: Doing my best when there is a job to be done.

    Caveats: After sharing this case story where the little boy makes an unwise decision, you can easily change it such that the little boy decides to make a wise decision. In the end of the story, the little boy would put all the pieces into the proper baskets.

    Follow-up Questions: Do you think the little boy felt good about the way he had done his job? Did the little boy show that he can be trusted from the way he decided to do his job?

Case Story: Once there was a little boy. He had spent the afternoon at an outdoor camp with his parents playing in the sand and mud, canoeing, and swimming. When they arrived home, his bag was filled with wet towels and dirty clothes. Mommy had taken care of the picnic, so her bag contained all the leftover food and dirty dishes. Daddy stayed outside to put the canoe back in the garage. Mommy asked the little boy, "Can you please put the dirty laundry in the correct baskets in the laundry room?"

The little boy knew what he had to do. They had three different laundry baskets, one for white laundry, another for light colored clothing, and one more for dark pieces. "Yes, Mommy," the little boy said. He grabbed the dirty clothes and towels from the bag and took them to the laundry room. They were dirty and wet. He dumped them all in one of the baskets. He did not separate them.

Question: Did the little boy make a wise or unwise decision?

Category: Attitude issues
Case 26: Waiting to get two candies

Background: When I first learned about the Stanford marshmallow experiment, used to test if children had self-control, I was intrigued. The premise was simple; you can eat one marshmallow now, or wait and get two. The children who had been able to control the urge and wait to get two marshmallows turned out to fare better in their adult lives. Since the implications of the child's decision were far-reaching, and the idea simple, I thought it was perfect material for a case story. I changed the story a little and used it to familiarize Jupiter with the idea of being patient and choosing to wait to get what he wanted.

Big Idea: Willingness to wait often pays off later. Self-control starts small and has major implications in adulthood.

Caveats: In my case the little boy only has to say "no" one time when he decides to refuse the chocolate bar at the store. In the marshmallow experiment the child was left in a room by himself, the marshmallow in front of him for twenty minutes. Clearly, it is a more challenging situation than this case story. I decided to start simple, then alter the story a little to look more like the Stanford experiment.

Follow-up Questions: What did the little boy have to be able to do to make a wise decision?

Cases on Attitude Issues

Case Story: Once there was a little boy. He loved candy. He was at the grocery store with Mommy. They were at the cashier. Mommy was paying for the groceries. The little boy saw his favorite candy right next to the checkout counter. "Mommy, can we buy this chocolate bar?" Mommy looked at him and said: "We have those at home. You can get this one, or if you can wait, you can have two after dinner tonight for dessert." The little boy wanted the candy. He decided he could wait. "Okay, Mommy. I can wait."

Question: Was that a wise or unwise decision?

Category: Attitude issues
Case 27: Doubling the amount of candy

Background: This scenario is a step up from the prior case. I wanted to set up a situation where Jupiter could practice holding off from something to gain more of it at a later time.

First I told Jupiter this case story, then made the case story reality in his life. Usually Jupiter gets a mixed candy bag, and we watch his favorite cartoons while eating the candy. After sharing the case story with Jupiter, I made it happen. I gave him only half the candy he usually gets and told him if he watched the cartoons for twenty minutes and not eat any candy, I would give him two more bags. This way he would clearly win by restraining himself.

Big Idea: Showing self-control pays off.

Caveats: This scenario may sound too artificial, but we had fun with it.

Follow-up Questions: What did he do to help him wait? Did he think about the candies or the cartoon while he was waiting?

Cases on Attitude Issues

Case Story: Once there was a little boy. He was looking forward to watching a children's program while enjoying a bag of gummy bear candies as he usually did on Saturday evenings. That night, Daddy proposed something different, "Here is your bag of gummy bears. If you can hold off eating any for the first twenty minutes of the program, I will give you another bag of gummy bears. If not, then you just have your one bag."

The little boy wanted to start eating the candies right away. He had been looking forward to enjoying the candies all week, and now he would have to wait even longer. He was unsure about it. However, it would be nice to get an extra bag.

The little boy turned on the cartoon program, put the candy bag on the floor, away from his sight. He did not want to even touch it. The little boy focused on the cartoons. When Daddy came back in twenty minutes with an extra bag, the little boy had not touched his candy bag.

Question: Was that a wise or unwise decision?

Category: Attitude issues
Case 28: Never give up

Background: This is a case to illustrate a most basic idea for little children. Every child has experienced trying to build or put something together when it keeps falling apart. It is easy to get frustrated and give up, or get frustrated and start calling for help. I have used many simple case stories about putting something together for a play and keeping at it even though it seems not to work. I just change the project under construction in the case story and tell pretty much the same event. The child tries to build something, and it keeps falling apart. I have advocated not giving up, but to keep trying. Asking help when nothing seems to work is alright, but calling for it after a few failed tries not so wise.

Big Idea: Never give up.

Caveats: The alternative is to share a case story where your child gives up, throws a fit, or starts throwing the construction pieces around. However, I try to convey the way of the mind in the non-quitter's process more than the quitter. It is easy to learn how to quit. I prefer to keep those examples to a minimum, only enough to get Jupiter to verbally acknowledge the foolishness of such choices. This case is easy to alter, the tower simply falls when the little boy puts the top layer on and the little boy gets angry and throws the blocks all around the room.

Follow-up Questions: How many times do you think he could try before giving up? When do you think he could give up? What if it just keeps falling, what could he do instead of giving up?

Case Story: Once there was a little boy. He loved building castles with blocks. The blocks he was using were not Legos, so the little boy had to balance them on top of each other just right to make the structure stand.

One day he was trying to build a tower as high as the table top. He had built the tower almost to the table top three times already, only to have it fall down right before making it. The little boy was getting frustrated. He started wondering if he was ever going to make it work. He also paid attention to what happened right before the tower fell. He noticed that the tower would start leaning toward one side too much before it crashed. He wondered if he should pay more attention to making the tower straight up from the beginning. He did. Every layer of blocks he placed on top of the previous layer, he made sure that the top layer was straight and the tower so far was standing balanced. He stayed calm and focused. He was almost at the table top level. He looked to make sure the tower was straight. It was leaning a tad to one side. The little boy decided to put the last two layers slightly to the other side to balance the structure. It worked.

Question: Was that a wise or unwise decision?

28. Cases on Sibling Disputes

Category: Sibling disputes
Case 29: It is not fair

Background: It is hard to be completely fair with everything between our children, at least from their perspective. One of them sometimes feels he got the short end of the stick. Assuming the parents are not favoring one child over another, children need to learn to deal with perceived fairness or lack of it. Life is not going to be fair, and it will help the children to understand this principle when they are young. You can help by telling case stories about a little boy who sometimes feels he is treated unfairly, yet responds with grace and overlooks the offense.

   Big Idea: Life is not fair. What we focus on, we magnify.

   Caveats: When a child claims, "It's not fair," what he often means is that he does not like what just happened. Sometimes it has nothing to do with fairness. Another point I try to get across with cases dealing with perceived or real unfairness is that it pays off to focus on what we have instead of what someone else has. We cannot right every wrong and have to learn to distinguish what changes we can affect.

   Follow-up Questions: How do you think the little boy felt? What do you think he would have wanted to say? Should he have made a fuss about it?

Case Story: Once there was a little boy who had a twin brother. Although the two were attending the same school, they were in different classes. The little boy liked his teacher, so did the twin brother.

One afternoon the little boy and his twin brother were sitting in the hallway, waiting for Mommy to come and take them home. The little boy noticed the twin brother had a small paper bag with something inside. He asked, "What do you have in the bag?" The twin brother smiled, "My teacher gave me a sticker book for knowing all my math facts."

The little boy did not like it. He had known all the math facts, too. Yet his teacher had not given him anything. That was not fair. He wanted to get a sticker book, too. Their mommy and daddy always gave them the same number of the same things. If his twin got two cookies, he also got two cookies. The little boy started getting upset. Then he realized that his teacher did not give out rewards like that, ever. The twin brother's teacher was different. That was just the way it was. The little boy did not say anything at first. Then he said, "Good job!"

Question: Was that a wise or unwise decision?

Category: Sibling disputes
Case 30: Taking turns

Background: Taking turns with toys is often hard. Children fight over who gets to play with which toy. Certain toys are the favorites, and the flavor of the day changes. One day one toys is what everyone wants, the next day it is something else.

Big Idea: Give a turn and figure out something else to do, something even better.

Caveats: The stunning model response in this case stops many a little one on his tracks. I remember how Jupiter looked at me in disbelief when I told him this story, as if nobody would do what the little boy did in the case. True, it is not the natural response, but so it is with many of our responses to situations. The unnatural response is the unselfish one, the one where we let go. The natural response is to fight for our stuff. It shows not only that the little boy chose to make a wise decision by responding so well, but also that he did not let the twin brother's rudeness ruin his fun. The twin brother showing up and demanding the toys with which the little boy was playing was an invitation, in a way, to respond in kind. Yet the little boy did not. Not realistic? You bet it is. I have seen it.

Follow-up Questions: Who is in charge of the little boy's fun? The toy? The brother? The little boy? Does having fun depend on having a specific toy?

Cases on Sibling Disputes

Case Story: Once there was a little boy who had a twin brother. They liked to play with similar toys. They often had the same favorites and liked to play together. However, sometimes each preferred to play alone.

One day the little boy had set up a play with an airport toy. He was playing alone and having a good time. He was in the middle of his play when his twin brother showed up. He had been taking a nap. His belly had been hurting. The twin brother said, "It is my turn to play with the planes now. You have been playing with them for a long time."

The little boy wanted to finish playing. He decided he could play something else. He could make it even more fun. He was in charge. He said to his twin brother, "Okay, that is fine. I am going to play something else. You can take the airport and the planes. Or do you want to play with me, something else?"

Question: Was that a wise or unwise decision?

Category: Sibling disputes
Case 31: Wanting what another has

Background: This is an example of a case story I used to teach what fairness is and what it is not in our family. If I believe my fairness to children is to give each what he needs, not necessarily equal items at equal times, then cases in this spirit give opportunities to help children understand that principle and how to respond to the parents' decisions about who gets and what. This is an area as grey as they get, and it helps to have our own guiding principles on how we think about it. For me, acting consistently is easier once my position is clear.

Big Idea: Fairness depends on the perspective and the circumstances. Sometimes even when we do not agree, we have to accept.

Caveats: I encourage Jupiter to express himself politely with words if he disagrees with me. Often from these cases Jupiter might get the idea he is to accept quietly and say nothing to disagree, which is not what I want to communicate. So we talk about how the little boys could have expressed his ideas without losing his temper. Or I change the case such that the little boy politely disagrees, praising it the wise choice. This way my son hears how the little boy could disagree politely.

In some cases it is best to let the case sink in without further discussion, but at other times the message gets across the best when discussed in further detail. This case story was a fruitful source of conversation with my son.

Follow-up Questions: What could he have done instead?

Case Story: Once there was a little boy. He had a younger brother. The boys were at a shoe store with their mommy. The little brother's shoes were too small, and Mommy was looking at new shoes for him. There were some fancy shoes in the store! The pair Mommy was considering for the little brother was just like the pair one of the little boy's friends had. So nice! Suddenly, the little boy wanted a pair, too. Sure, the little boy's shoes still fit well, but they looked worn. He said to his mother, "Mommy, I want new shoes, too. Look how mine are worn." Mommy looked at the little boy's shoes and said, "They just look a little dirty. We can wash them. We will buy you a new pair of shoes when these become too small."

The little boy disliked what Mommy said. He wanted exactly the shoes his little brother was getting. He wanted them now. He got upset. He started screaming and threw a temper tantrum in the store.

Question: Was that a wise or unwise decision?

Category: Sibling disputes
Case 32: A comparison trap

Background: Somebody else will always have something that is better than what you and I have, or what our children have. For your child it could be more toys, a bigger room, a new dress, or the latest toys. My grandmother used to have a sampler on her wall that read, "Jealousy is the cancer of the soul." It has stuck with me. I have been vigilant about not allowing those little pieces inside of me. Cultivating jealousy is a sure way to bitterness and unhappiness.

I wanted to help Jupiter own the idea. We are wiser and happier when we are not jealous of another's possessions. We should be happy for someone when they are fortunate. We should appreciate and enjoy what we have, making the most of them the best we can.

Big Idea: Jealousy is a cancer of the soul.

Caveats: This case story is an opportunity to help your child to understand that even though we have ugly feelings, what matters is what we do about them. We learn to make decisions about how to respond. This case can be altered to end with the little boy demanding they switch the rooms.

Follow-up Questions: Was it all right to feel jealous? What did the little boy say and do to make it a wise decision?

Cases on Sibling Disputes

Case Story: Once there was a little boy. His family was moving to a new house. The little boy and his little sister were so excited because they would get their own rooms. They had been sharing a room in the old house.

One day Mommy and Daddy took them to see the new house. There was a big front yard and a forest behind the house. It looked like a fun place to play. When they entered the foyer, Daddy said, "Let's go upstairs. I will show you your rooms." The children followed.

The first room at the end of the staircase was the little boy's room. It had two windows facing the forest and its own bathroom. It was nice. He liked it.

Then they went to see the little sister's room. Wow. It was different. There was a built-in part that looked like a cave or a secret closet. Also, the little boy realized when he saw his sister's bathroom that he did not have a bath tub in his bathroom, only a shower. His sister clearly had a better room. The little boy felt jealous. He said, "Our rooms are different. She has a bath tub, and I do not. She also has a secret closet. Why is that?" Mommy looked at him and said, "Since she is younger, we thought she would need a bath tub more than you do. You are a big boy. You can take a shower instead of a bath." "Okay," the little boy responded. He decided to make his room the best room he had ever had. He did.

Question: Was that a wise or unwise decision?

29. Putting It Together

Making every-day events into case stories

Putting it together means you begin engaging your child with the cases. You do not need to carry this book around and read cases from it. Rather, after reading through them, you should have an idea how simple they are and how you make them up from simple, everyday scenarios, from the child's perspective. The following two illustrations show how you could take an event and make a case story about it. Could you imagine yourself in the following story?

Example 1: Evening case story about an earlier incident

You have had a busy day at work and just picked up your three-year-old Paula and six-year-old Sophia at their after-school programs. The girls seem happy but tired. Sophia asks if she can play a game on your phone. You are fine with it so you say, "Sure," and hand her your phone.

Paula throws a fit, "I want to play, too! It's my turn!"

You feel exasperated and are just about to say something when Sophia responds, "That's all right. You can have it. I can take a look at the books I just got at the library."

You are stunned. Paula had already played with the phone that morning, so it was not her turn. Yet Sophia had simply let it go. "Thank you, Sophia. How nice of you," you say to her. Paula takes the phone and starts playing with another app. Sophia seems pleased and pulls out one of her library books from her schoolbag.

The evening goes as usual. Sophia goes to her soccer practice with her father while you stay at home with Paula. At bedtime you read a couple stories for the girls. Sophia picks the first story, and Paula picks the second one. When it is time to wrap up the reading, the incident in the car comes to your mind. You decide to try a case about it.

You start, "Listen to this before we call it a night." You decide to use the girls' favorite characters from *Frozen* and proceed, "Once there were two sisters, Anna and Elsa. They loved each other. Anna was younger, almost four. Elsa was the big sister. She was six years old. They both liked playing games on their mother's phone. They had a rule about it. They were only allowed to play games on the phone when they were either in the car or waiting at the doctor's or the dentist's office. One afternoon Elsa, the older one, asked for the mother's phone while they were driving to school in the morning. Of course, Anna, the little sister, wanted to play, too. Elsa stopped. She thought about it. She could do something else. 'Okay, Anna, here you go. I can look at one of the books I have.' Elsa gave the phone to her little sister and pulled out a book from the front seat holder."

You pause for a moment for effect, then continue, "What do you think about that? Did Elsa make a wise or unwise decision letting it go? Not arguing?"

Your daughters look at each other. Then Paula says quietly, "Wise."

"That's right," you affirm her.

Sophia smiles. She knows right away it was a story about what had happened earlier. You continue and address the younger child, "You are right, Paula, Elsa made a wise decision when she decided to let it go and not argue. She chose to do something else instead, and make that the fun thing to do instead. Good job! What do you think Sophia?"

Sophia smiles again, "She made a wise decision."

You drive it home by praising the wise choice, "You two know how to make wise decisions. It is hard to do. You have to be able to let go. Great job."

You kiss both girls and hug them, "I love you so much. I am so glad you know what it means to make wise decisions."

With this case story you have driven home the positive side of the incident. The positive was that your older daughter, Sophia, had been able to let go of what she wanted to do at first and change to something else. The negative was that your younger daughter, Paula, had claimed for herself something the older one had started doing first, whining and begging. You decide to let that go for now. Even if Paula does not say a word about it, it is all right. She will remember and connect the dots at some point. Let *her* do it. Give her the opportunity to add it up in her head and do the finger pointing herself. She will do it.

There are countless other ways your daughters could have responded to your case story. No matter, you keep it simple and focused on the dilemma in the case, the decision to give up the phone. You engage them about the choices they make every day. You pay enough attention during the day to recall events, change them into a case story, and then let your children evaluate the behaviors by posing a question.

You ask questions to promote thinking instead of make statements that create resistance. For example, you could have exclaimed, "Paula, what you did today in the car was bad manners." An alternative is for you to tell Paula a case story about a little girl who constantly wants to have what her sister has. At the end of the case story you ask Paula to evaluate. You let Paula save face and not address Paula's transgression in front of Sophia by making a comment about Paula's unwise manners.

Example 2: Pre-emptive strike against going with the foolish crowd

In another illustration, imagine your son, Jack, is about to start kindergarten. You have talked to him about the new friends he will meet at school and perhaps even about choosing friends. You have talked to him about listening to the teacher and doing what the teacher asks him to do. Most of the time Jack knows what is right and what is wrong, even if he does not always do the right thing.

However, you want to help him to stand alone and do the right thing even when it is hard and the others are doing the wrong behavior. To facilitate this, you would like to tell Jack a case story about something that might take place at school in the coming days. In every schoolyard there are children up to mischief. You ponder what that could look like in kindergarten.

The next morning while you are having breakfast with Jack, he wants you to read one of the *Star Wars* storybooks. After you finish the story, you recognize an opportunity to make a quick case story about Luke Skywalker, Jack's hero from the story you just read to him. You ask him, "Would you want to hear another story about Luke Skywalker?"

So you share your case story. "A long time ago, when Luke was only six years old, he was in kindergarten. He was learning to read and worked hard on his handwriting. He liked learning. Every day at school they had playtime and recess. That was his favorite part of the school day. One day Luke was outside playing with Biggs, his best friend at school. They were playing at the school playground at recess. Some boys from another class joined them at the monkey bars. One of them was talking to Biggs. Luke was unsure what they were saying at first. Then Biggs came to Luke and said: 'Luke, come! They are going to show us how to spit at the windows.'

"'What? Spit on the windows?' Luke responded. He knew it was not the right thing to do. Luke didn't want to be left out and was a little intrigued. It might be fun. Biggs asked again. Since Biggs was Luke's best friend, he considered for a second to go with them, but the sense this was wrong was more powerful. *Luke stopped to think.* He would not go.

"Luke said to Biggs, 'Biggs, those boys are trouble. I am not coming.' Biggs ran off with the other boys. Luke turned around and decided to climb up the monkey bars again.

"Did Luke make a wise or unwise decision?"

Jack gets it. He knows the answer. "Wise decision," he answers, smiling.

"What a wise boy you are! You know wise from unwise! Great job!" You praise him and continue, "Do you think it was easy or hard for Luke to do that?" Jack responds, "Hard, because his friend Biggs went with those boys." You kiss Jack, you praise him and hug him.

With the simple case story you have *pretend-walked Jack through a likely event at the playground*. It is probably not going to be about spitting when he goes to kindergarten; however, Jack will be challenged in the coming days at kindergarten to walk away from some kind of unwise decision. The case stories referring to those situations help your child put himself in that position of making that choice before it happens in his life. They help him live through that process, imagine some of the pressures, yet be able to make a wise choice easily in the case. Cases like this, speculating on possible future events that might take place, help your child to open up pathways in his thinking to move in the wise direction.

You know the miracle when you see it

The case method miracle takes place when your child starts making mindful wise decisions in his own life, both in situations that resemble told case stories and in situations that do not. By no means do the cases work their miracle after you have shared one or two cases with your child. However, once you, as the parent or the caregiver, make it a habit to incorporate them into your conversation and experiences with your child regularly, they will start to activate the miracle. The miracle takes place when your child finds joy in making wise decisions in his own life, on his own, without anyone's prompting. The miracle also takes place when his wise-decision-making transfers to unrelated areas beyond the scope of any cases you have ever told him. The miracle takes place when your child perseveres to follow through with what he believes is wise, when he has developed grit not just about tasks but ideas and beliefs. The miracle takes place when the child is upping his game to be true to what he believes is wise.

Putting it together means you begin engaging your child with the cases. You understand the premise and the key assumptions behind the approach. You have confidence to tell the simple stories and to tailor the approach to fit your family. Inevitably glitches come along the way. You will have failures and victories. To be successful we have to celebrate our victories and learn from them and our mistakes. What did I do right, what did I do wrong? It is a learning process like everything else in life. I am convinced the case method is the simplest, yet most powerful approach to teach self-reliance and grit to our children. Or perhaps instead of using the word "teach," I should say "usher in" self-reliance and grit. The most important part of the case method miracle is to start doing it, and start simple and start small, learning along the way about your children and yourself.

IV.

Troubleshooting:
When Things Go Wrong

The unexamined life is not worth living.
Socrates

30. Obstacles to Starting

You may have reservations about trying the case method approach—as I have defined it—with your child. In this chapter I share some hesitations I have heard and how I would address them.

"It is too much work, I do not have time for this."

Each hour of the twenty-four you have is taken up by something. Some of it you get to decide, some you do not. You have to constantly prioritize. You also have to prioritize how you spend the time you have with your child.

Engaging your child in one-on-one give-and-take is a choice that pays dividends for the rest of your lives, for him and for you. Engaging your child with the case method to accomplish the miracle will bring happiness and wisdom into your lives and relationships with your child.

Even if the miracle comes slowly, you will still gain benefits from engaging and bonding with your child. Taking the risk to try it will only contribute, not take away from a good life. You can make it as little or as much work and time as you choose, there is no rule about it. The bottom line: it doesn't take long. We are talking single-digit minutes! But the payback is in hours, days, and eventually, a lifetime.

"I have several children. How do I do it?"

The more children you have, the more significant the benefits of the case method. Isn't it better to have children that are self-reliant than who need you all the time for every little issue? Isn't it better that you can trust them to make wise choices instead of worrying about them?

Also, siblings tend to look at each other for behavior models, so once you get the wisdom quest implanted even in one of them, the momentum will start building on its own, without any extra effort from you. In business we call it economies of scale. As I described in the story of Sophia and Paula in the previous chapter, sometimes you can tell a case story to two children at one time, maybe three. Then they learn together and from each other. You just have to be aware and avoid the comparison trap.

"It is hard to find one-on-one time with each child, I cannot be in two places at the same time. Does it work if I tell case stories to all of them at the same time?"

The one-on-one engagement works most effectively when the case stories are focused on that particular child's individual experiences and behaviors. For example, retelling as a case story a wise decision you observed your child make.

However, most of our children's experiences are quite universal. Some examples include how to greet other people, how to be kind when a friend is hurt, how to have good table manners, how to show appreciation, and similar common issues. I do not see a problem sharing some of the more universal stories that apply to your entire offspring when everyone is present. You will have to balance the rewarding with individual and group praise.

On the other hand, you can use the moments you have one-on-one to address and share scenarios pertinent to a particular child. The case stories do not take long. Remember to keep them short, about a minute or so.

"I am not a storyteller."

Nobody is born a storyteller. It is a developed skill. Everyone can improve their imagination and storytelling abilities.

The simple case stories are perfect to build those skills. Start with reading the examples in this book. Once you have read through them, describe a simple scenario where your child makes a wise choice.

Your children are the most forgiving and encouraging audience when it comes to telling stories. Continue to build your skills, delight your children, and enjoy the ensuing benefits. If you goof up, laugh it off and try again. Your child won't mind.

"My child is strong-willed and often seems to argue a different view just to disagree with me."

You may be surprised, but by design, the case method is most suitable for your strong-willed child. What kind of students are accepted to Harvard Business School? Those with strong wills and opinions, those who move forcefully and have strength of character. I dare say most of my peers at Harvard Business School, if not all of them, were strong-willed as children.

Sure, you have constant power-struggles with your strong-willed child, because he wants to do it his way and make his own decisions. However, isn't that what you eventually want for your child to do, as long as those decisions are wise and good? So what you have to do is to use the case method stories to guide and nudge him towards wisdom and good decision-making. That is what the professors do at Harvard Business School. They just have about ninety of those strong-willed kids in their mid-twenties battling it out in the same room.

Due to the strong-willed child's desire to have his own way and opinion count, I suggest you try cases where you end with an open question. The older your child, the better the open ended questions work. You tell a scenario with a little boy facing a dilemma of sorts, but not knowing what to do. You may even act a bit as if you are not quite sure what he should do either. Since your child "knows" everything, let him show you how he knows wise decisions for the little boy in the case, too. Your child will own what he comes up with. Then you praise him for being so smart and wise to solve the dilemma.

Your strong-willed child is usually self-motivated and driven. He not only wants to make his own decisions, but then goes after what he wants with vigor. The pressure is on you to use the third person case scenarios to urge your child to conclude and then to want to go the right way, thinking it his own way. You have a diamond in the rough with your strong-willed child. What a perfect setup for the case method miracle!

"My child wants to know the rules to break them, not keep them."

The case method is not tailored to a certain type of child, whether a rule-keeper, rule-breaker, or something else. The approach appeals to your child's desire to be loved, to engage with you, and to stand-alone.

The way a child responds to the case stories initially varies. You see how your child responds on the outside. However, what happens on the *inside* is the key. For some children it takes longer to start assuming the wisdom stand, but it is not a reason to give up. Maybe your child will use the case moralities to test his limits and try his boundaries. It is impossible to predict and manage the behavior of each child. You simply try the approach, see what happens, make adjustments, and try again. There is power in the approach, power we cannot see.

To illustrate, Ms. Amanda, a nanny to three-year-old Elsie, had shared a case story with Elsie about a little girl who had taken her markers and drawn on the wall. Elsie correctly identified that the little girl made an unwise decision by drawing on the wall. Ms. Amanda thought she was preventing such an incident from happening by helping Elsie see it was unwise.

Unfortunately, as if on cue, Elsie took her finger-paints the next day and painted on her furniture. Apparently, Elsie had chosen to take the unwise action she had learned about in the case story and do it herself, perhaps to see what would happen. Ms. Amanda confiscated Elsie's paints. There was not going to be any painting with them until Elsie showed she can be responsible to make real-life wise decisions.

Ms. Amanda continued to tell case scenarios to Elsie and whenever she caught Elsie making a wise decision, she pointed it out and hugged her, praising her for the choice.

The idea of the case method is to sink in the *desire* to make wise decisions. The love rewards help in that regard. It is wise to figure out what kind of rewards work the best to communicate love to your child. The desire to be loved trumps many others.

In summary, if you do not try this approach, you will never know if it works or not, or how it works. You will not see the case method miracle. If you try it, put yourself out there with your child, you may experience what I have described. You cannot lose. Aren't you curious?

31. Common Issues and Possible Solutions

Tailoring the approach is essential

At its core the case method with young children is easy to do. Anyone who can talk can implement it. You do not have to be a child development expert, a psychologist, or even a Harvard graduate. However, calibrating the case method as I have described it to *your* situation will likely take some trial and error.

As you start on the journey using the case method with your child as a parent or a caregiver, being observant and present is the key to the success. It is what helped me over a number of years to define and express the basic elements of the approach. Sometimes the approach was working, then it was not, and then it was again. I paid attention, pulled back, and made some adjustments.

When I shared with some friends I was using the Harvard Business School case method with Jupiter, they got curious. I gave examples and walked them through the basic structure of a case. Receiving feedback from others doing case method with their children helped me further understand the key elements to make it work and some common pitfalls. I also concluded that what worked in our family did not always work in other families and vice versa.

Start here for potential solutions to common dilemmas

As I listened to the dilemmas other parents raised about the case method and how they had tried it, I recorded some of the conversations.

In this chapter I share a few of these stumbling blocks and possible solutions. If the proposed solutions do not make sense to you about your issue, it may make sense to review the ground rules and see if you have diverged from them in a significant manner. Also, this is more art than science, and what works for one child may not work for another. In any case, perhaps some of these shared experiences point you to an idea that works.

Dilemma 1: The child resists. "Not one of those again!" "Can we do something else?"

Potential issue and solution: Frequency. How often are you doing them? Consider starting slow, doing rather too little than too much. The idea is for your child to desire "wise and unwise decisions" or whatever it is you are calling them. Take a break from cases for a while, and start again. Maybe try one on a slow Saturday night, then another one a week later. Build with the positive case examples.

Potential issue and solution: Positive and negative balance. Check if you are using the cases to point to your child's wrongdoings. If you are, try to do more positive cases. Positive cases are those when your child not only knows the wise choice for the case protagonist but also realizes that he has done the same wise behavior himself. The case acts as an affirmation for something he has previously done. Your child feels good about knowing the answer and his own action.

Potential issue and solution: Setting. Check the setting where you engage your child with the cases. Is there too much lecturing? If your child feels he is being lectured about his faults each time you start telling a case story, you may need to re-create the atmosphere. Is the setting mutually bonding with loving atmosphere? Consider sitting close and holding your child. Consider what your child would enjoy.

Dilemma 2: The child is not interested.

Potential issue and solution: Rewards. Is there something in it for him? Are you rewarding your child with meaningful, love-communicating rewards? Hardly any child will initially be baited and hooked to the case stories by simply "learning wisdom." Try the rewards you think best express love and acceptance to your child.

Potential issue and solution: Characters. Who is your case protagonist? A generic little boy or girl may work for some children, but many want to hear about their heroes. Who might that be for your child? Or is there a surrounding your child likes? Perhaps you could make the cases take place in that venue?

Potential issue and solution: Distractions. Is the setting taking away from focusing on the story? Is the child still emotionally tied to the case event? Is it too close to the event when waiting to later would work better? Are there too many children involved?

Potential issue and solution: Humiliation. Sometimes it is better not to have all the siblings together listening to a story, especially if the case is bringing out an incident with an individual child. Are you exposing your child to being humiliated before his siblings?

Dilemma 3: The child seems to get confused and not know the answer.

Potential issue and solution: Simplicity. How many actions are there to judge in your cases? Check to see if you are bringing more than one issue to bear per case. If you have several issues in a case, try making it a serial case where you ask questions along the way or split the story into several stories. Simple is better than complicated in getting into the habit of choosing wisely. Check also how elaborate your story is. There is no need for coloring it beyond the key elements bearing on the case.

Potential issue and solution: Length. How long are your cases? Try to stay at about one minute. Most of mine are less than a minute. Focus is key. If you get lost in the story, your child probably will, too.

Potential issue and solution: Perspective. How much are you telling your side of the event versus your child's perspective? None of how mommy or daddy feels or what they are thinking belongs to a case description. The child is making a decision with what he knows and perceives about the event.

Dilemma 4: There seems to be no natural time to bring up the cases.

Potential issue and solution: Priorities. How much downtime do you have with your child? Do you have times to connect with each other? Try building that kind of margin into your family schedule.

Potential issue and solution: Segue. Do you have a few minutes between activities that you could use to connect with your child? Openings during which you might be tempted to connect with your friends, could you capture those for your child instead? The case story times do not have to be significant stretches dedicated to stories, they can as easily be moments in between. Remember, these are minute-long scenarios. You can transition from a finished activity to a case story without too much interruption. You could use something like, "While we were … I saw something… Could I put it into a case story to see what you think about it?" You want to stay away from gossip or slander, so no names, and try to also notice exemplary behavior.

Potential issue and solution: Pull. Keep in mind that the transition to the cases is smoother when your child is eager enough to hear the case stories. If there is enough pull from your child, then as you offer a case story, he should be up for it most of the time. Check if you are perhaps pushing the case stories too much as teaching moments, your child immediately recognizing them as such? Does your child seem to read you trying to make a point? Then the fun of it may not be there for him anymore.

Try the cases in settings disconnected from any behavioral training or lecturing. An idea other than a dedicated story time is to steal a few minutes while in the middle of something. You pull your child aside, as if telling him a secret, making it a special "you and him" moments.

Dilemma 5: The child is not owning the issue in his life.

Potential issue and solution: Identification. Try to make sure your child puts himself in the shoes of the case protagonist. Is the case protagonist easily identifiable for your child? Can he easily imagine himself as the case protagonist? If not, then choose a different character for your cases. Even better, ask your child who he wants the case character to be.

Potential issue and solution: Relevance. The case issues may not be relevant to your child. Are your cases describing what your child experiences?

Potential issue and solution: Transfer. Many moral fairy tales have what is called the transfer problem. This refers to the child knowing the story but not applying the moral lesson in his own life. The cases are not moral fairy tales. They are specific about one issue, short and simple to that point, and the key is that your child pictures himself in the role of the case protagonist. Your child becomes the ruler for the case protagonist. This is why it is imperative that your child identifies with the case protagonist and that the scenarios resemble your child's own experiences.

Potential issue and solution: Tell and do. Is there a gap between what you am showing to be wise and what you am modeling for your child? Maybe it would help to explicitly catch yourself doing the unwise behavior, make a show of it, and then share what to do about it. It helps to show your own vulnerabilities and gives the chance for your child to show grace to you, the parent or the caregiver.

Potential issue and solution: Responsibility. This issue calls for self-examination. Are you trying to push your child to correct behaviors you have created? Does he have a choice? What part do you play in the issue? Is your behavior the root cause of the problem? Also, are you pushing extreme compliance over compliance? Perhaps you need to give your child a chance to do it his way instead of expecting immediate compliance your way.

32. Acknowledgements

When I started molding the Harvard Business School case method approach to fit my needs for teaching my three-year-old son wise decision-making, it did not occur to me to write a book about it.

I owe it to Mark, my husband, and Leslie Gilbeaux, my friend, that I ever began writing this book. It was their encouragement and observations that convinced me to write down what I was doing and how I was doing it. Every night, Mark would read what I had written that day and offer his feedback. Every day, Leslie would discuss with me the concepts about which I was writing or help me collect example cases. If Socrates had left a treasure on the road for me to pick up, then Mark and Leslie were the ones to help me shine it to be presentable.

I gained ideas about the book structure and the writing process from Calvin Edwards who offered his time to give feedback on my progress. I am also thankful to him for the many edits he offered to improve my manuscript.

So many friends helped me by giving feedback about the idea, editing the manuscript, explaining the book publishing business, or trying my approach with their children. Thank you, Natalie Aide, Frank Benevento, Taryn Bowman, Denise Danpierre, Illya and Armando Del Bosque, Donna Cook, Jill Dixon, Abby Elmore, Brooks Heiser, Greg Hiebert, Lara Hodgson, Ross Mason, Jeff Rayport, Debra Rosumny, Ann Schoenberg, Alison Stone, and Elizabeth Yaniglos.

Jupiter Jones, my son, was amazing in going though the case stories, making sure I had kept them clear and simple. He made some great edits!

Finally, thank you to Harvard Business School for the two years I spent there to gain my first exposure to the case method. I knew I would benefit from having learned to make better decisions in business, but I would have never expected to use my business school education so directly to become a better parent!

33. About the Author

Anne Ylipahkala Jones grew up in Kiviniemi, Finland matriculating at the top of her class from one of the most successful educational systems in the world. The Finnish schooling is not based on testing and teacher control, but on both teachers and students taking responsibility. The Finnish school structure aims to produce independent learners, emphasizes broad knowledge, and teaches morality from a young age. Growing up in this kind of educational environment had an impact on Anne's views on training up children.

Trying her wings in the United States, Anne ran track on a full athletic scholarship at Georgia Tech in Atlanta, Georgia, and graduated with highest honors in systems engineering. She worked in performance improvement consulting prior to receiving her MBA from Harvard Business School. Before retiring from the corporate world, Anne worked for over ten years holding progressively senior positions in finance, strategy, and organizational effectiveness with NYSE companies including Southern Company and Mirant in Atlanta. The year Anne met her husband she had deliberately left her fulltime corporate job for a part-time consulting gig to allow her time to date and perhaps meet that special man. She did.

During the early marriage years, Anne and Mark revitalized Mark's surgery business. Anne was able to apply what she had learned in the professional world to help the family business. With a baby in her arms, Anne, ever the engineer who seeks to be deliberate about her life, sought effective ways to raise a wise son. This is how she developed the way to use the Harvard Business School case method to train children in wise decision-making.

Anne, Mark, and their youngest son, Jupiter, reside in Buckhead, a neighborhood in Atlanta, Georgia.

Made in the USA
Middletown, DE
02 November 2020

23190406R00130